WHITE FUNNELS

The Story of P&A Campbell Steamers 1946-1968

Chris Collard

The author aboard the Ravenswood, *passing the English & Welsh Grounds lightvessel, in the summer of 1950. It was a memorable afternoon for the five-year-old, for reasons explained in the introduction.* (W.T. Collard)

WHITE FUNNELS

The Story of P&A Campbell Steamers 1946-1968

Chris Collard

For my wife, Rosie, my son, Alex and all those who have known and loved the White Funnel steamers.

TEMPUS

First published 2001

PUBLISHED IN THE UNITED KINGDOM BY:

Tempus Publishing Ltd
The Mill, Brimscombe Port
Stroud, Gloucestershire GL5 2QG
www.tempus-publishing.com

PUBLISHED IN THE UNITED STATES OF AMERICA BY:

Arcadia Publishing Inc.
A division of Tempus Publishing Inc.
2 Cumberland Street
Charleston, SC 29401
(Tel: 1-888-313-2665)
www.arcadiapublishing.com

Tempus books are available in France and Germany
from the following addresses:

Tempus Publishing Group
21 Avenue de la République
37300 Joué-lès-Tours
FRANCE

Tempus Publishing Group
Gustav-Adolf-Straße 3
99084 Erfurt
GERMANY

British Library Cataloguing in Publication Data.
A catalogue record for this book is available from the British Library.

ISBN 0 7524 2147 6

Typesetting and origination by Tempus Publishing.
PRINTED AND BOUND IN GREAT BRITAIN.

Contents

Acknowledgements

During the first forty years of my continuing research into the history of the White Funnel Fleet, I have been fortunate enough to have received considerable help from many people. Some of them are, sadly, no longer with us but I wish to pay tribute to the late Ivor Ashford; Fred Birmingham; Howard Davis; Ernest Dumbleton; Maurice Evans; Grahame Farr; Fred Plant; Stan Galley; Jack Guy; Cyril Hawkins Garrington; Cyril Goodall; Leslie Hansen; Jim Hendry; Olwen James; Edwin Keen; Graham Langmuir; Stanley Miller; Colin Morrow; Dr R.V.C. Richards; Capt. L.G.A. Thomas; Francis Thompson; Ernest Vivian Tucker and Howard Woodberry.

I would also like to acknowledge the help of Associated British Ports; Newport Museum and Library; Cardiff Public Libraries; Swansea Industrial & Maritime Museum; Ilfracombe Museum; Woodspring Museum; The Public Records Office; *The Bristol Evening Post*; *The South Wales Argus*; *The Western Mail & Echo* and *The Swansea Evening Post*; Dr David Jenkins of the former Cardiff Industrial & Maritime Museum; and the personnel of P&A Campbell Ltd. Of the latter I wish to mention in particular Roy Barclay, former Second Engineer; Syd Gray, former Chief Steward; Captains George Gunn and Phillip Power; Alan Wakeman and Peter Southcombe.

Special thanks are extended to Mr John Williams BA DAA, Bristol City Archivist, and his staff at the Bristol Records Office, especially Miss Alison Brown whose willing assistance in my continuing research is much appreciated; and to the numerous friends and acquaintances, many of them fellow members of the Paddle Steamer Preservation Society, who have played such significant parts in contributing to this history, particularly Richard Clammer, Nigel Coombes, Viv Davies, Ken Jenkins, John Kelly BEM, Alec Lewis, Patrick Murrell, Seaton Phillips, John Ruddle, Mike Tedstone, Phillip Tolley, Lionel Vaughan and Gordon Wood; also to Terry Sylvester of Waverley Excursions Ltd.

To several people I owe a particular debt of gratitude: to my father, William T. Collard, for taking me on my first boat trip; to John Brown and Sydney Robinson for allowing me to scrutinise, at length, their meticulously maintained scrapbooks; to the Revd Norman Bird, for sharing with me his factual records and extensive reminiscences from his White Funnel sailing days; Dr Donald Anderson, former Chairman, now Secretary of the Bristol Channel branch of the Paddle Steamer Preservation Society, for contributing his eminently evocative foreword, for setting me on the road to research many years ago, and whose support and stimulation continue to be highly valued; and finally to Mr George Owen, the leading authority on Bristol Channel matters. His breadth of knowledge, expertise, and meticulous researches in the pursuit of historical accuracy have been a shining example. His friendship and unfailing help are an inspiration.

Foreword by Dr Donald Anderson Secretary, PSPS (Bristol Channel Branch)

Chris Collard describes 'White Funnels' as the definitive history of the White Funnel paddle steamers from the end of the Second World War to their demise in 1968. The claim is a bold one but there are few more qualified to make it. A naturally enquiring mind, coupled with a near obsessional determination to get at the truth, has given the author the necessary credentials to investigate his subject in the finest detail. Resisting the temptation merely to regurgitate the pontifications of other writers in the field, he has taken his enquiries back to the source – to the log books of the steamers and the company records of the time – to produce this immaculately researched account.

From the ordinary reader's point of view I suppose a criticism could be that a learned thesis of this kind leaves little scope for painting 'word pictures' of the atmosphere of the times. Younger readers are left unaware of the fun we 'old stagers' derived from such simple pleasures as counting the number of steamers upon which we could sail in a day, and the complexity of our timetable planning to achieve the highest total. And then there were the 'up at dawn' preparations for silent, early morning journeys on the single-decker trolleybus to the Pier Head in Cardiff. We would embark on some ridiculously timed sailing, geared solely to the tides and in complete disregard of commercial viability. At the other end of the day we might come ashore for a pint in the Big Windsor Hotel with company Traffic Manager Jack Guy. An even later, after closing time, return could be the signal for a somewhat guilty visit to Sam On Yen's restaurant in 'naughty' Tiger Bay.

Such late night adventures usually had their beginnings in a jostling contraflow with the dust-blackened firemen trundling their convoys of outrageously overladen wooden coal barrows on the pontoon ramp to and from the steamers. *Ravenswood*, *Glen Usk* and *Glen Gower* would be bunkered with frenetic energy by men desperate to beat 'stop tap' in the pub. Full size 'Hornby look-alike' coal trucks, with such famous names as *Ocean*, *Powel Duffryn* and *Lewis Merthyr* on their sides, loomed vaguely from the dense cloud of coal-dust which invariably surrounded them in their siding.

Of the ships themselves, I wonder what memories will be evoked amongst the author's older readers? A Campbell steamer had a magic of its own. I bring to mind narrow-planked, varnished decks and similarly varnished gangways. The latter were not nearly so wide as their aluminium counterparts on *Waverley* today. I see the canvas weathercloths stretching back amidships along the rails from the bow and recall them as a helmsman's nightmare when they filled with wind as he tried to come alongside a tricky pier. In my thoughts I hear the occasional 'canon-snap' and visualise the whiplash of three-inch hemp hawsers, unable to take the strain like today's pleated nylon ropes. Below decks I am carried back to the spartan dinginess of the wooden-seated forward saloons of the pre-war survivors of the fleet and to the rather grubby steam-misted glass screens which surrounded the engine room and impaired my vision of the crank shafts whirling around. How small and powerfully compact the two-cylinder compound diagonal engines of the pre-war steamers appeared in comparison with the triple expansion magnificence of the *Queens*. And how intriguing was the Fairfield patent 'clickety-clacking' of the unique valve gear of the *Cardiff Queen*.

I was a proud young man sitting on the tool box alongside Chief Engineer John Taylor on the control platform of the *Glen Usk*, deep in serious 'steamer talk', and I felt no less privileged to enjoy one of Chief Steward Vic Taylor's steak and chips long after the dining saloon had been closed to ordinary mortals.

In those crucial 1950s years why, I wonder with hindsight, did not the much vaunted business acumen of Mr Smith-Cox cause him to ponder the archaic, and latterly somewhat tarnished, silver service catering arrangements and introduce instead a cafeteria-style, swift throughput facility? Why, though souvenir shops were a feature of most other steamers, were Campbell eyes blinded to their potential beyond a few postcards from under the tea lady's counter? Why were 'off service' days protected as virtually inviolate even though, on some occasions, a switch of day would have enabled a steamer to operate on a far more profit-worthy schedule?

Forty years ago the steamers still provided a transportation service for holidaymakers and their baggage, in particular to Ilfracombe and, latterly, to Butlin's Camp at Minehead. This required some sort of regularity in spite of tidal inconvenience. It often involved the departure of sailings at the most inhospitable hours. In consequence, much valuable day excursion traffic was sacrificed merely to keep the goodwill of the period return passengers. Gradually, over the years, the latter journeyed by other means but it was a long time before the company could bring itself to abandon pointless early morning starts and non-connecting late finishes. I recall particularly some of these strangely timed calls at Penarth when, perhaps with only one or two passengers to embark or disembark, the steamer would glide alongside the pier for the gangway to be slid ashore and the passengers hustled across. Then the ship would pull away again without a rope ever being cast.

Government imposed safety standards restricting rough weather sailing were far less of a constraint thirty to forty years ago. It was rare indeed for a voyage to be cancelled in the face of forecast heavy seas. Immune to the indignation of storm-weary officers and crews, we regulars revelled in the excitement of braving the elements, albeit soaked to the skin. Lack of investment and inadequate maintenance may indeed have played their part in the chronicle of mechanical catastrophes to boilers, engines, and paddle wheels, which are a regular feature of this book. However, no one can deny the battering those ships received when the Bristol Channel threw down its gauntlet of gales and mountainous seas.

The captains, braving all weathers on the open bridges of those days, would marvel at the array of modern technology aboard the present *Waverley*. Not for them were the luxuries of pinpoint navigation, of radar, of depth sounders, and ship to shore telephones to tell their wives to put the kettle on for tea. Their navigational skills were in their bones. Capt. Findlay Brander, in his kid gloves, swayed rhythmically to the thrust of the engines as he calmly nudged alongside a storm-lashed Birnbeck Pier at Weston-Super-Mare. He was guided by a current indicating 'batman' precariously clinging to the landing stage and by his own intuitive 'left hand down a bit' to the helmsman. Subtle Jack George, like a latter day 'Mr Wot', peered grimly over the canvas dodger as his ship was steered close inshore to pick up the last advantage of the flooding or ebbing tide. Jack Harris, like a bat out of hell, set his course in a straight line, rang down 'Full Ahead' and flinched not an eyebrow until his destination was reached.

Playing with memories is a dangerous game. Chris Collard's story is about my heydays as the ultimate 'steamer nutter' and about the steamers I shared with a band of enthusiasts just as crazy as myself. If they were around today I have no doubt that they would be jostling to read *White Funnels* and to join with me in thanking the author for his efforts and wishing him well.

Introduction

On a Sunday afternoon in the summer of 1950, a small boy stood with his father on the foredeck of the White Funnel steamer *Ravenswood*. She had sailed from Newport and was now passing the English and Welsh Grounds Light Vessel, on the way to Clevedon and Bristol. The five-year old boy was already a seasoned Bristol Channel traveller and was familiar with all of the White Funnel steamers – except one! For some reason the *Cardiff Queen* had always eluded him and consequently, in his eyes, she had acquired an aura of mystery and fascination.

As the *Ravenswood* sailed down the River Avon on the return trip, the boy heard, in the distance, a long blast on a chime whistle; undoubtedly another Campbell steamer was approaching – could it be the *Cardiff Queen*? The boy ran to the bow in a state of feverish anticipation as the *Ravenswood* approached the next bend. He heard the faint tinkle of an engine room telegraph – the advancing steamer was slowing down. Then, at last she appeared – it was the *Cardiff Queen*! She approached slowly and passed so close to the *Ravenswood* that one could have almost shaken hands with her passengers. What a magnificent and awe-inspiring sight she was as she steamed gracefully past, with her huge paddles turning slowly and plumes of hazy smoke rising from her two gleaming white funnels. The fellow captains exchanged a cursory wave, the briefest of acknowledgements so that their concentration on the navigation of that difficult river was not disturbed. She continued her dignified progress up-stream and was soon out of sight.

But not out of mind. The incident had a profound effect on the youngster and marked the beginning of a lifelong passion for the White Funnel steamers. That afternoon he determined that he would find out all that he could about them and, one day, write their history.

Although many years have now passed, in recalling that occasion the feelings of excitement are as strong today as they were on that Sunday afternoon in 1950.

I was that boy!

Prologue

The origins of P&A Campbell's White Funnel Fleet of paddle steamers lie in early nineteenth century Scotland, when the Campbell family began its steamer services on the River Clyde. In the 1880s a series of events led the brothers, Peter and Alexander, to transfer their business from Glasgow to Bristol where, despite intense competition, they quickly established themselves as the major pleasure steamer operators. As the popularity of marine excursions flourished in the 1890s they increased their fleet, extended their network of Bristol Channel services and ventured into a new enterprise on the south coast of England.

The Golden Age of the paddle steamer ended abruptly with the outbreak of the First World War when, in common with most other fleets of excursion ships, the Admiralty requisitioned the thirteen Campbell vessels, principally for minesweeping.

At the end of the hostilities the company recommenced its peace-time services, which continued throughout the difficult years of industrial unrest and the Depression, until the outbreak of the Second World War, when the Admiralty, once again, requisitioned the entire fleet, which then consisted of eleven vessels.

Only four of those paddle steamers survived to sail again, but after the gradual resumption of sailings in 1946, and with the delivery of three new steamers, the company enjoyed a number of profitable seasons during the early post-war years.

In the 1950s, however, the company's fortunes went into decline; partly as a result of its own practices, which failed to keep pace with the changing demands of the public; and partly as a result of rising costs, the increasing trend towards private motoring, and one bad summer after another.

Although the company was saved from demise in 1959 and continued its services for a further twenty-one years, economic pressures enforced the disposal of the last of the paddle steamers in 1968.

This account of the company's post-war history touches, only briefly, on the broader issues of management and finance. It is concerned, principally, with the activities of the steamers themselves, and has been meticulously researched over many years from a wide variety of sources. In this respect it is hoped that it may be considered definitive.

The aims of the book are simple – to enable those who have known and loved the paddle steamers to relive their memories of a bygone era and to introduce younger generations to the excitement and sense of adventure experienced in sailing on the Bristol Channel.

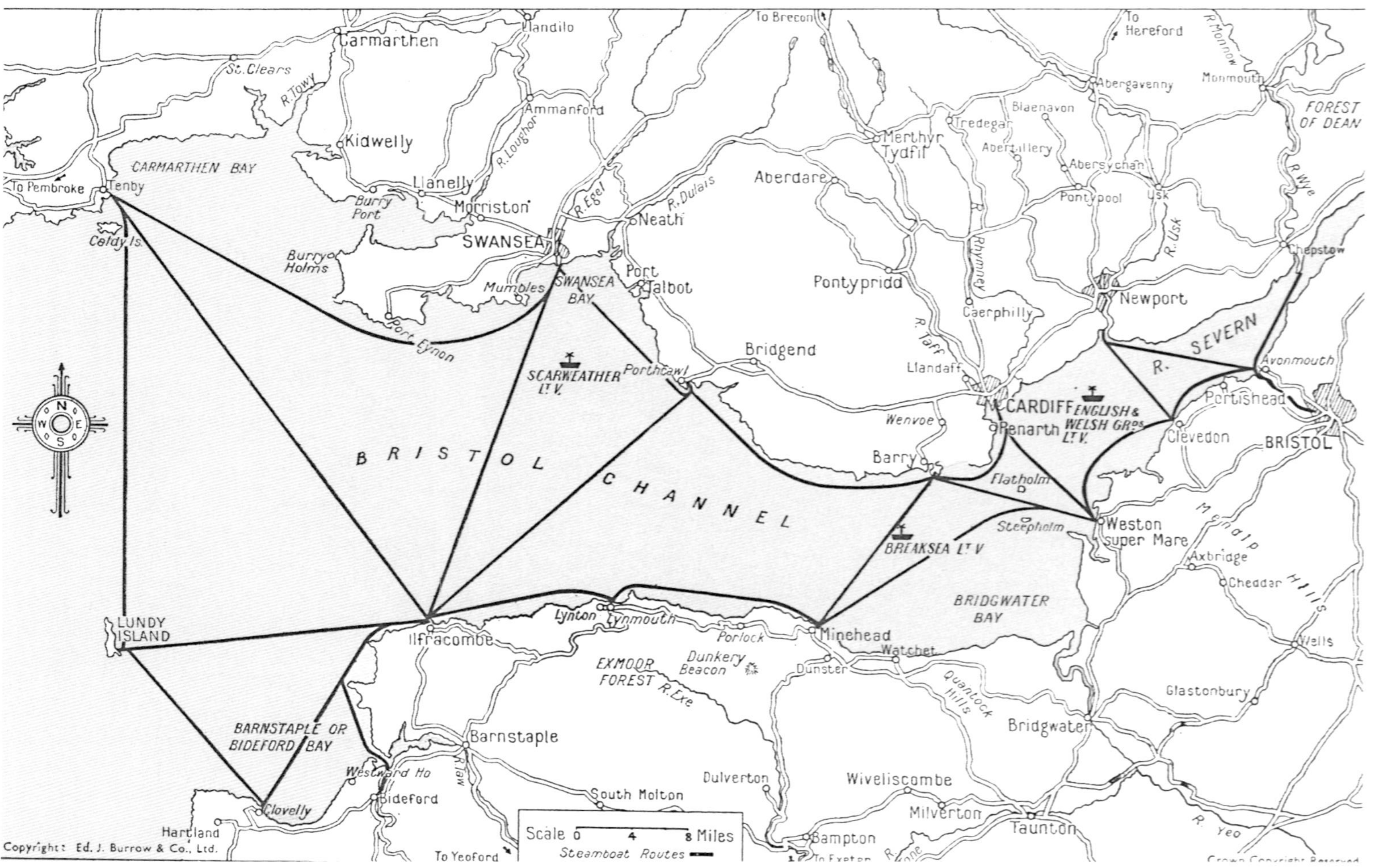

The Bristol Channel routes from The White Funnel Handbook.

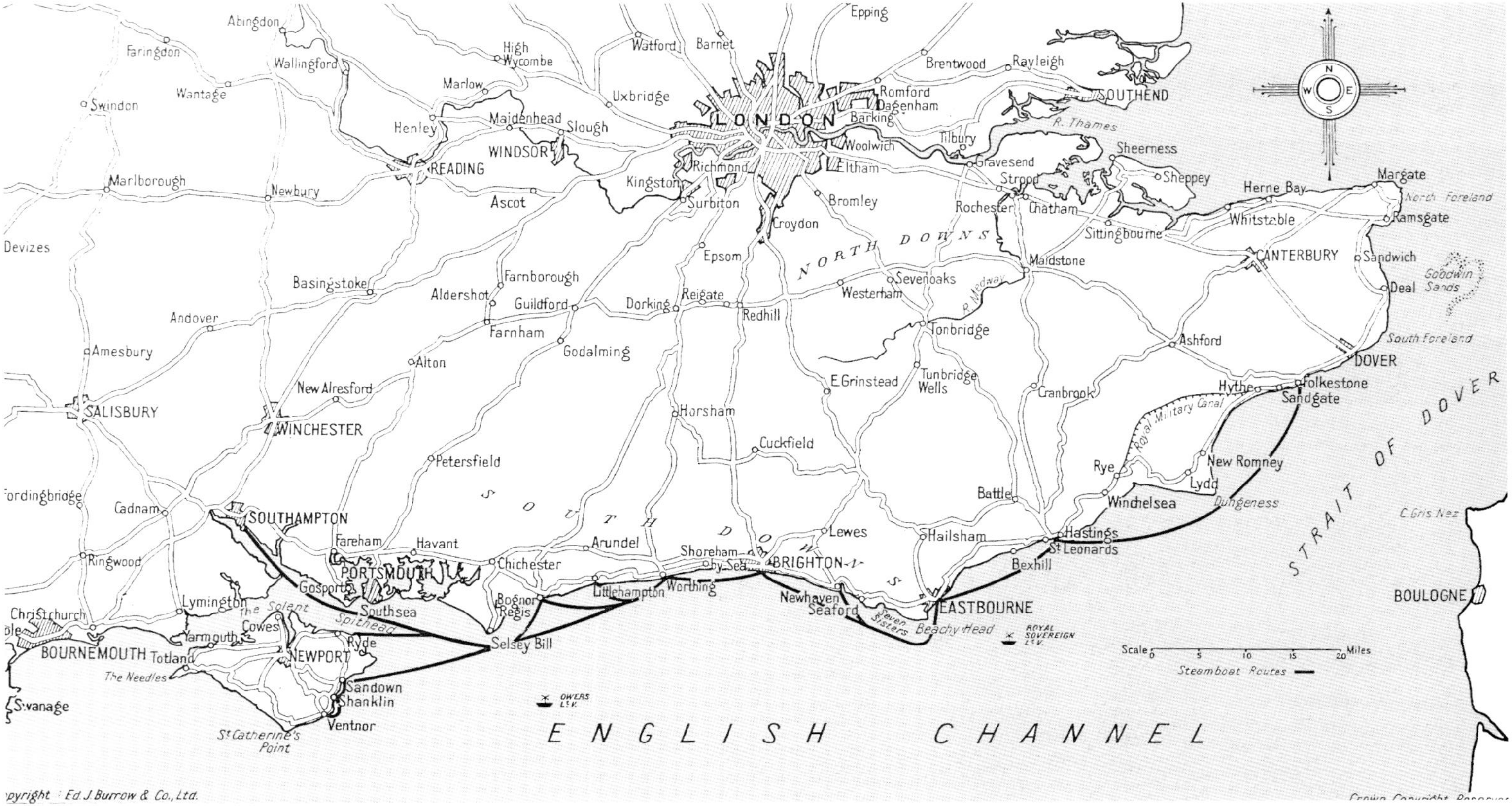

The South Coast routes from The White Funnel Handbook.

1946 – New Ships For Old

As the Second World War drew to its close in early 1945, and Allied victory became more certain, the management of P&A Campbell Ltd considered the future of its seriously depleted fleet of excursion vessels, and the replacement of at least some of its war casualties. Of the eleven paddle steamers owned by the company at the outbreak of the war, the *Brighton Queen*, *Brighton Belle* and *Devonia* had been lost during the evacuation of Dunkirk. The *Waverley* had been sunk during an enemy air raid in the North Sea, and the *Glen Avon* had foundered in a storm in Seine Bay, off the French coast. The *Cambria*, in London, and the *Westward Ho*, at Dartmouth, were both in use as accommodation ships and looked most unlikely to sail again. The turbine steamer *Empress Queen*, requisitioned on completion of her building in 1940, was in the hands of the Ministry of War Transport and engaged in troop carrying duties between Stranraer and Larne.

A blueprint has come to light since the war which shows the general arrangement of a vessel 230ft long by 31ft breadth. She was to be built either as a coal or oil burner, with a service speed

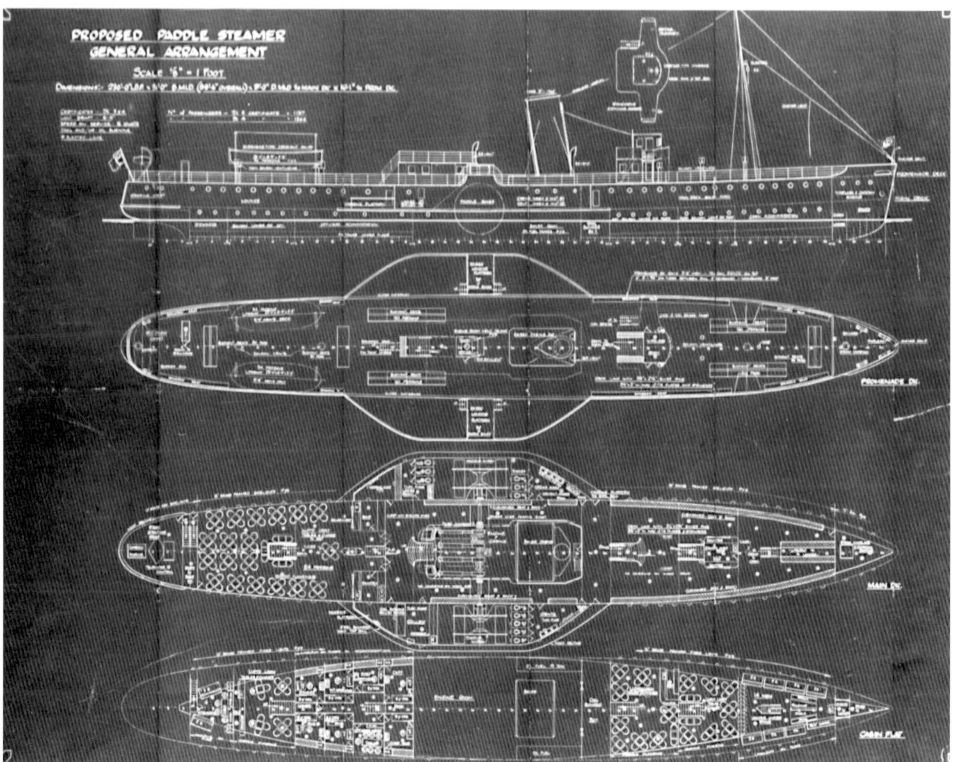

The general arrangement plans for a proposed paddle steamer; such a vessel or vessels never materialised.

of sixteen knots and a maximum passenger capacity of 1,350. The small engines and paddle wheels indicated that economy of operation was to be one of her principal features. Neither the date of the drawing nor its origin is known, so whether or not it illustrates the proposed new steamers of that time is uncertain, but in any event, such ships never materialised. The two steamers built for the company in the post-war era were larger and of quite different design.

The order for the first of those steamers was placed on 4 April 1945 with the Bristol shipbuilders, Charles Hill & Sons Ltd. They subcontracted the construction of the boiler, engines and paddle wheels to Rankin & Blackmore, of Greenock, and it was hoped that delivery would take place in May 1946.

The four paddle steamers which were destined to resume passenger service returned to their home port of Bristol during 1945. The first to arrive was the *Ravenswood* on Monday 9 April, followed by the *Britannia* on Thursday 17 May, the *Glen Gower* on Monday 25 June, and the *Glen Usk* on Wednesday 3 October. They were taken in hand by Charles Hill & Sons Ltd for refitting.

An article in the *Bristol Evening Post* on Friday 18 May 1945 stated:

> ***Ravenswood getting ready. Trips in July?***
>
> *After an absence of over five years the familiar house-flag and ship decoration of the White Funnel Fleet will probably be seen in the Bristol Channel early in July.*
>
> *She has emerged from dry dock and just above her present waterline can be seen the familiar foundation of the well known colour scheme that, in peace time, adorns all the ships of the fleet.*
>
> *Transformation above and below decks is proceeding rapidly and, so far as Messrs. Campbell are concerned, the* Ravenswood *will be ready to take her former place on the Weston to Cardiff ferry service in the second week of July.*

Rankin & Blackmore's three-crank, diagonal triple expansion engines prior to their installation in the Bristol Queen. *The cylinders were 27in, 42in, and 66in in diameter, with a stroke of 66in, and took steam at a pressure of 180lb psi. from a double-ended Scotch boiler, 15ft diameter and 18ft 6in long.*

The Ravenswood *steaming down the River Avon on the first post-war trip. Saturday 13 April 1946.* (Edwin Keen).

The article concluded by stating that the re-opening of the service was, however, 'contingent on certain circumstances over which the company has no control.' This comment, no doubt, referred to the shortages of materials and manpower, which delayed reconstruction and precluded the resumption of sailings that year, despite strenuous efforts on the part of Hill's.

The *Ravenswood* was, however, the first steamer to re-enter civilian service. Under the command of Capt. Findlay Brander the first post-war passenger sailing – a cruise down channel to off Clevedon pier – left Hotwells Landing Stage, Bristol, at 15.33 on Saturday 13 April 1946 with a full complement of passengers, including civic dignitaries, company shareholders and

The Ravenswood *in the Avon Gorge, returning to Hotwells Landing Stage after the first post-war trip. Saturday 13 April 1946.* (Edwin Keen).

invited guests. The queue of intending passengers extended for a considerable distance along Hotwells Road from the landing stage, many of whom had to be left behind.

After the *Ravenswood* had returned to Bristol she left Hotwells again at 18.55 for a single trip to Cardiff and narrowly avoided a mishap on the falling tide during the crossing. The log book records:

> *20.15 English & Welsh Grounds Lightship close on starboard beam.*
> *20.30 Ship dragging heavily and touched bottom on bank extending NW of East Cardiff Buoy. Damage, if any, unknown.*

However, she berthed at Cardiff at 21.20 apparently none the worse for the experience.

On the following day, Sunday 14 April 1946, she made the first sailing from Cardiff – an afternoon trip to Bristol with a cruise to Walton Bay, and on Tuesday 16 April 1946 ran the first trip from Newport – an evening cruise down the River Usk towards the English & Welsh Grounds Lightvessel.

She then settled into a pattern of sailings calling at Cardiff and Penarth, Bristol and occasionally Newport; a somewhat limited service imposed by doubts as to the safety of Clevedon pier and the poor condition of Weston Super Mare's Birnbeck pier. However, both resorts were reopened on Thursday 23 May and Thursday 6 June respectively. Calls at Barry pier had been resumed on Good Friday 19 April.

Behind the scenes, in the early post-war months, the company's plans for the future continued to forge ahead. On Thursday 20 December 1945 the Managing Director, Mr William James Banks, had reported to the Board of Directors that Charles Hill & Sons Ltd and the Ailsa Shipbuilding Co. Ltd, of Troon, had been asked for a quotation for the construction of a second

The first post-war call at Newport. The Ravenswood *leaves on a cruise to the English & Welsh Grounds lightvessel. Tuesday 16 April 1946.* (Chris Collard Collection).

new paddle steamer, to be delivered by the beginning of the 1947 season. Neither company, however, could meet this deadline owing to pressure of work.

On Monday 25 March 1946 Mr Banks wrote to the Fairfield Shipbuilding Co. Ltd, of Govan, Glasgow, 'I had a trip about three weeks ago in the PS *Jupiter* and I was very much impressed with her general lay out and the machinery. I am wondering whether you could quote us for a similar ship.' (Fairfield's had built the Clyde steamer *Jupiter* in 1937). On Friday 10 May 1946 Mr Banks reported to the board that Fairfield's had submitted a satisfactory tender, and in view of the fact that no other shipbuilder could guarantee delivery for the 1947 season, he had verbally accepted their offer. This was, in turn, sanctioned by the board and the building of the second new post-war steamer began.

Towards the end of May 1946 the *Britannia's* refit was completed. Her first passenger sailing took place on Saturday 1 June 1946 when she left Bristol at 08.37 for Clevedon, Cardiff, and the first post-war call at Ilfracombe. As she lay alongside Ilfracombe pier the Chairman and Members of the Council were welcomed aboard by Mr William Gerard Banks, son of the Managing Director, for the afternoon cruise to off Lynmouth; the Civic Party and residents alike delighted to see the resumption of passenger sailings to their resort.

The *Britannia's* sailings over the following weeks followed a similar pattern – Bristol and Clevedon to Ilfracombe via either Weston or Cardiff, Penarth and Barry. Apart from the *Ravenswood* being out of service from Wednesday 19 June 1946 for a few days, because of boiler trouble, this state of affairs continued for just over six weeks, but then changed drastically.

On Friday 19 July 1946 the *Britannia* had spent the day on the Cardiff to Weston ferry. She had finished her sailings for the night at 22.20, the passengers had disembarked and only the crew

The Britannia *leaving Bristol on her first post-war trip, and the first post-war sailing to Ilfracombe. Saturday 1 June 1946. It was appropriate for the* Britannia *to perform this duty; having been the last steamer to call at the north Devon resort, on Sunday 3 September 1939 – the day war broke out.* (Chris Collard Collection)

The Britannia *in the Avon. June/July 1946.* (Chris Collard Collection)

remained aboard. In the log book, for Saturday 20 July 1946, Capt. Brander recorded:

> *00.50 While lying along side Cardiff pontoon, in the Burnham berth, a muffled thud was heard by me. I arose at once and upon opening the door of my room, observed steam escaping. Upon enquiry from the Chief Engineer I was informed by him that there had been an accident to the boiler. Later, when the Chief Engineer was able to enter the stokehold, he reported several boiler stays were fractured. Other damage, at present,unknown.*

For those on board, most of whom were asleep in their cabins, the experience was somewhat frightening; the lower decks were filled with escaping steam and were permeated by considerable heat. The ship's Chief Steward, Mr Syd Gray, recalls:

> *I closed the fire doors and helped to get everyone out. All the varnish in the lower bar, which was close to the boiler room, was blistered, and the heat was so intense that all the rims came away from the glasses which were racked above the bar. Fortunately no one was hurt.*

She was withdrawn from service and on the evening of Saturday 20 July the tugs, *Victor* and *Royal Briton* towed her from Cardiff to Bristol, where she was moored at the company's Underfall Yard to await her fate.

The *Britannia's* 'Haystack' boiler had been installed in 1935. This particular type of boiler was, at that time, somewhat outdated, although it did have certain advantages. In design it consisted of a circular furnace area, around the circumference of which were the furnace doors. Above this was a circular 'pan' which covered the whole furnace area and which supported the numerous boiler tubes encased in a vertical, circular cylinder, consisting of an inner and outer shell. This was surmounted by a dome; thus, the whole structure resembled the shape of a haystack. The great virtue of this type of boiler was its rapidity in raising steam, the pan over the furnaces heating up very quickly; but this was where very heavy wear occurred. The average life of a haystack boiler was twelve to fourteen years, depending on how hard the vessel was driven. In the case of the *Britannia* this was hard enough in peace-time but during her war years she had been driven harder still and received much less maintenance.

P&A Campbell Ltd maintained that the *Britannia's* boiler failure occurred as a result of her war service and a claim for compensation was submitted to the Admiralty. The company's report stated that when the vessel was taken over by the Government in October 1939 the Admiralty surveyor found the boiler in very good condition. The report continues:

> *During her war service the vessel was subject to severe shocks from the explosion of mines very close to her.*
>
> *The boiler was carefully examined by the Ministry of War Transport and owners representative before returning to the owners' service, when only two stays and several pan nuts were found to require renewal. Pan nuts being a normal renewal as they burn away.*
>
> *On the night of the incident the Chief Engineer was awakened by the foreman of the coaling gang and he tried to get to the boiler room by way of the engine room, but was unable to do so due to escaping steam until a half hour had elapsed. On examination the inner shell was found to have collapsed inwards at a height of about 5ft above the line of firebars, to a depth of from eight to ten inches. The position of the bulge was between the centre forward and port forward furnaces. From this examination a number of stays between the inner and outer shells were found to be broken, whilst others were pulled through the shell plate, allowing the water to escape.*
>
> *At the time of the explosion a coalman was in the forward coal bunker and escaped through the coaling scuttle.*
>
> *The explosion was caused by the failure of the aforementioned stays. The failure of one or two stays would allow the inner shell to flatten inwards imposing a greater load than normally carried, on the adjacent stays, causing these to fracture and so on progressively until the inner shell collapsed.*
>
> *The unusually large stayed area of the inner shell in this type of boiler is not designed to withstand any sudden increase and diminution of pressure, such as would occur when a mine exploded close to the vessel, and such shocks would inevitably result in fractured stays. Considering the narrow space between the inner and outer shells, a fractured stay in the middle of the collapsed region would be difficult to detect.*
>
> *Had the vessel continued for six weeks longer under steam in the Government service, it is evident that the explosion would have occurred then. Therefore we claim that the defect was latent in the boiler when handed back to the owners and being the outcome of war service we have the right to claim compensation.*

This unfortunate occurrence led to a hasty re-scheduling of certain sailings, and the temporary cancellation of all the down channel trips. Fortunately, however, the *Glen Usk*, refitting at Charles Hill's, was rushed into service within a week of the *Britannia's* boiler failure. She left

Bristol for Cardiff on the afternoon of Wednesday 24 July 1946 with Capt. George Clifford Spong in command and took over the *Britannia's* sailings from the following day.

In addition to refitting three of the White Funnel steamers in just over a year, Charles Hill & Sons Ltd completed the building of the first post war paddle steamer and new flagship of the fleet less than eighteen months after the laying of her keel; remarkably efficient work considering the shortages of material and manpower after the war.

The *Bristol Queen* had been launched at 14.30 on Thursday 4 April 1946, exactly one year to the day since the contract for her building was signed. 3,000 people attended the ceremony, which was performed by the Lady Mayoress of Bristol, Mrs James Owen. A bottle of Bristol Milk sherry, which failed to break at the first attempt, was used for the purpose. Lieutenant (Engineer) Alec Campbell and Mr R.J.T. Campbell, sons of the late Capt. Peter, were present; the former having arrived in Bristol in the early hours of that morning following demobilisation from the Royal Navy.

The *Bristol Queen* was the largest of all the White Funnel paddle steamers with a gross tonnage of 961.39, length of 258ft 5ins overall, and a breadth, over the paddle boxes, of 59ft 9ins. With its raked stem and cruiser stern, her hull shape had been designed following the results of the tank testing of a 17ft model by the National Physical Laboratory at Teddington. This was an innovation for the company, as were the oil-fired boiler and the three cylinder triple expansion engines. Her two funnels, sun lounges forward and aft, and two lifeboats on the after promenade deck gave her much top hamper, which, combined with her shallow

The Bristol Queen *being launched at the yard of Charles Hill & Sons, Bristol, on the afternoon of Thursday 4 April 1946. On the right is the* Britannia, *undergoing her post-war refit.* (Edwin Keen)

March 6, 1947 SHIPBUILDING AND SHIPPING RECORD 227

In order to determine the best possible lines for the "Bristol Queen" a self-propelled model was run in the Teddington tank

Right: The model paddle wheel

Centre: Stern view of the model hull

Below: Model condition corresponding to ship loaded condition at a speed of 17 knots

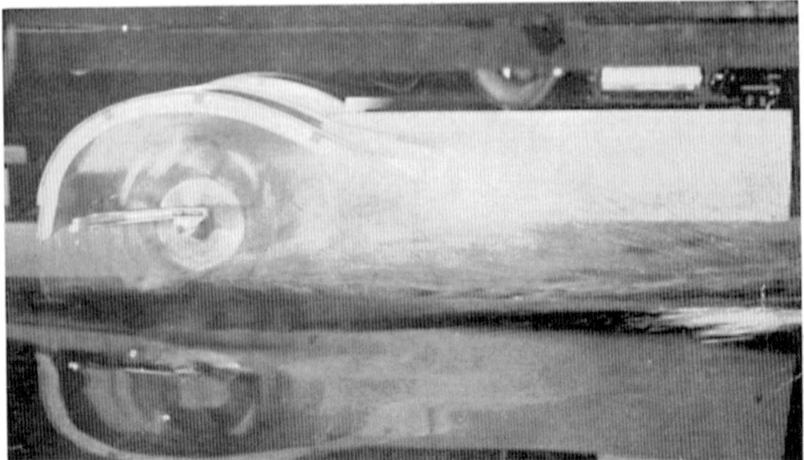

Illustrations included in a report on the building of the Bristol Queen. *Part of the report stated, '...estimates were taken by the National Physical Laboratory for the shaft horsepower required, allowances being made for the air torque of the paddle floats and the friction in the feathering mechanism. It is intended to take records in the forthcoming season to correlate the model results to the ship. The conditions in service so far have confirmed the tank estimates.'*

The Bristol Queen *fitting out at Charles Hill's yard, Bristol. Sunday 28 July 1946.* (H.G. Owen)

draught, made her somewhat difficult to steer in a cross wind. However, she made an impressive sight gliding slowly down the Avon, with the aid of a tug, on the afternoon of Saturday 7 September 1946, the date set for the start of a series of trial trips. Her sailing orders for that weekend were as follows:

> Saturday 7 September 1946.
> *Ship is to be ready to leave the shipyard at 14.00. High water is 17.14 and the Harbour Master requires the ship at the Junction Lock by 14.15. He expects that she will be able to leave the Cumberland Basin at approximately 15.15. One tug has been ordered to attend the ship from the shipyard to the basin, but to take no line from the ship until leaving the locks at the Cumberland Basin unless requested by the captain of the* Bristol Queen. *A compass adjuster has been arranged for Saturday afternoon and on clearing the mouth of the river the ship will proceed to a suitable spot for adjusting compass. During and after compass adjusting engines will be run at various revolutions to suit engineers. After compass adjusting and during daylight hours the ship to return to Avonmouth Pier entrance for the night of Saturday/Sunday. Particulars of crew on board will be arranged by Mr Coles in conjunction with the acting captain, (Capt. J.A. Harris), and acting engineer of the ship.*
>
> Sunday 8 September 1946.
>
> *Trial party to embark at Avonmouth New Pier by 10.30. During the day official trials will be made, circle turning, steering gear, astern running and anchor trials included. The ship will proceed to Bristol on the evening tide and tie up in the berth she vacated on Saturday.*

With her fitting out almost complete, the finishing touches are put to the Bristol Queen *as she lies at the Mardyke Wharf, opposite Hill's yard, on Thursday 5 September 1946. Her brass chime whistle has yet to be fitted.* (Edwin Keen)

On the Saturday the sailing orders were followed, as the log book entries show:

> *14.20 Dep. Hill's fitting out berth. Tugs* John King *and* Volunteer.
> *15.00 In basin. Dock Pilot (Murphy) in charge.*
> *15.33 Dep. basin. In tow – tug* John King.
> *16.55 Out of river and cast off tug and proceeded to swing for compass adjusting.*
> *18.32 Finished adjusting and entered South Pier, Avonmouth, secured for the night.*

However, on the following day proceedures did not go according to plan:

> *11.05 Departed Avonmouth South Pier.*
> *11.20 Engines stopped and picked up tug.*
> *11.24 Tug* John King *secured and proceeded back to Avonmouth.*
> *12.22 Slipped tug and proceeded alongside South Pier.*
> *14.00 Secured Avomnouth.*

Why the scheduled trials did not take place has never been fully explained. A brief, pencilled note in the memorandum book simply states 'knock in LP', which indicates some kind of engine trouble, but no further details have been found. In fact, at intervals throughout her career a prominent 'knock' could often be heard emanating from her engines which, however, appeared to cause no problems.

The Bristol Queen *leaving Bristol for trials. Saturday 7 September 1946. During the course of further trials two days later, a message was flashed to the ship from the Walton Bay signal station – 'Floating tree in channel near Portishead Point. Please report if sighted'. The* Bristol Queen *flashed back – 'Have just passed floating tree and sighted another. Position' etc. Such obstructions could, naturally, have caused untold damage to the paddles.* (Ernest Dumbleton)

She entered the locks at Avonmouth early on the morning of Monday 9 September to take on fuel, sailed at 10.15 and headed down channel. At 12.15, off the Breaksea Lighvessel, she stopped for engine adjustments but shortly afterwards proceeded for steering gear and anchor trials. During the latter a defect was noted:

> *15.30 At anchor in Walton Bay. Anchor would not leave hawse pipe readily due to insufficient clearance over lip of anchor box. Defect remedied by builders later.*
> *17.30 Anchor weighed and proceeded to Bristol.*
> *21.03 Secured at fitting out berth.*

The speed runs are not recorded in the logbook but probably took place after weighing anchor at 17.30. The company's records give the following details:

> *Two speed runs attempted from the Nore to Battery Point. A distance of 1.2 nautical miles.*
> *First run-up with tide. Time: 3mins 50secs (Campbell)*
> *3mins 47.3secs (Hill's)*
> *Mean: 3mins 48.75secs for 1.2 miles = 18.885 knots.*
> *Second run-down against tide. Spoiled by slow down by shallow water and running on to course in a curve.*
> *Time: 3mins 16secs for 1.2 miles = 13.670 knots.*
> *Total: 32.555 knots for 2 runs. Mean speed 16.277 knots.*

Over the years many exaggerated claims have been made as to the speed of the *Bristol Queen*, especially that attained on her trials. As can be seen from the above she did not run official Board of Trade trials, i.e. six times with and six times against the tide on a measured mile, but only two runs, one of which was not a fair test, and which did not give a true indication of her speed. Hill's specification stated 'Speed 18.5 knots light and 17 knots loaded, on a measured course.' It is perhaps best that the last word on the matter should be that of the late John Taylor, Senior Chief Engineer of P&A Campbell Ltd for many years, who said of the *Bristol Queen*, 'We could get nineteen knots out of her for a short burst of five to ten minutes duration, but she could not sustain it.'

Her maiden trip took place on Saturday 14 September 1946 when she left Bristol at 09.17 and sailed, in a strong westerly wind, slight sea and light rain, direct to Ilfracombe, where she arrived at 13.15. Her first calls at Clevedon and Weston were made on the following day, at Cardiff and Penarth on Monday 16 September 1946, and at Newport and Barry on Tuesday 17 September 1946, all of the calls being made on her way from Bristol to Ilfracombe.

During her first week in service she met with some wild weather, which culminated in her sailings being cancelled on Friday 20 September 1946 because of a southerly gale. She also encountered a number of minor mechanical troubles, most of which were rectified without disruption to her timetable. Only one days sailings had to be cancelled on Wednesday 25 September 1946 because of a breakdown in the forward capstan. Otherwise she ran well, on the route for which she had been intended, i.e. Bristol to Ilfracombe, via either Weston or Cardiff, Penarth and Barry, until her last trip on Sunday 6 October 1946.

The Bristol Queen *leaving Bristol on her maiden trip, to Ilfracombe, Saturday 14 September 1946.* (Chris Collard Collection)

The Bristol Queen *approaching Ilfracombe pier, having anchored offshore to allow the* Glen Usk*, seen in the background, to embark her passengers for the return trip to Weston, Penarth and Cardiff. The* Bristol Queen *then embarked her passengers for her return trip direct to Bristol, Saturday 14 September 1946.* (Edwin Keen)

The elegance and power of the Bristol Queen *are shown to their full advantage in this broadside view of her as she steams at full speed past Battery Point, Portishead, on her way down channel to Clevedon, Weston and Ilfracombe. Sunday 15 September 1946.* (Edwin Keen)

The Bristol Queen, *seen from the Clifton Suspension Bridge, heading down the Avon Gorge on a cruise to Walton Bay, on the afternoon of Sunday 22 September 1946. This view shows the considerable amount of after deck space taken up by the two lifeboats; a defect which was to be remedied a few years later.* (Edwin Keen)

The *Ravenswood* had retired for the winter on Monday 23 September 1946, leaving the *Glen Usk* to close the season on Monday 7 October 1946.

So ended the first summer of the post-war era. It had not been an easy season because of the limited resources. Calls at Swansea, Porthcawl, Lynmouth, Clovelly and Lundy had not yet been resumed; the piers at Mumbles and Tenby were out of commission and Minehead pier had been completely demolished. Nevertheless, the company provided the best service possible. In fact, there had only ever been two ships in service at one time, except for just over a week after the *Bristol Queen* began sailing. The trips were, however, well patronised and the trading profit for the season amounted to £57,930.

Aboard the Glen Usk *at Hotwells Landing Stage, Bristol, in 1946.* (Cyril Hawkins Garrington)

1947 – Piers and Problems

The year of 1947 brought extremes of weather, the very fine summer being preceded by an appalling winter, the winter of the 'Big Freeze'. From January until mid March, most of the country experienced heavy snow and sub-zero temperatures. The ensuing disruption to transport led to severely limited fuel supplies, widespread power cuts, and compounded the already serious problem of food shortages. Nevertheless, work began on the preparation of the White Funnel steamers for the forthcoming season, except the *Britannia* which was still laid up at Bristol – the cost of replacing her defunct boiler then being the subject of negotiations between the company and the Admiralty.

The season was opened on Thursday 3 April 1947 by the *Ravenswood*, with Capt.G.C. Spong in command, and the *Glen Usk*, with Capt. W.F. Watson, on the following day.

On Thursday 17 April 1947 the *Ravenswood* acted as a tender to the Shaw Savill & Albion liner *Wairangi*, taking her passengers and their baggage into the Queen Alexandra Dock at Cardiff. The 'Western Mail' of the following morning reported the details:

> *The first food ship to enter Cardiff since the Minister of Food's promise to Mr L.J. Callaghan, MP for Cardiff South, of food cargoes for South Wales ports, arrived in the roads yesterday morning. She was the* Wairangi, *from New Zealand, carrying 8,500 tons of meat, cheese and butter and about 1,000 tons of sundry cargo. Also aboard the ship were 107 passengers who were disembarked by the steamer* Ravenswood *and left for London later in the day.*

During the following week there was a considerable disruption of sailings. On Monday 21 April 1947 the *Glen Usk* was taken out of service for repairs to her boiler. A strong SW gale was blowing which increased in force on the following day causing the *Ravenwood's* evening sailings to be cancelled. By Wednesday 23 April 1947 the gale had worsened and the *Ravenswood* remained at the Pier Head, Cardiff, for the whole day.

By Thursday 24 April 1947 repairs to the *Glen Usk* were completed but her sailings were cancelled because of the continuing bad weather. On that day the *Ravenswood* made her way to Bristol to lay up for a few weeks before Whitsun, leaving the *Glen Usk* to maintain the Cardiff to Weston sailings alone, on her return to service on Saturday 26 April.

Less than a week later the weather deteriorated again and on the evening of Friday 2 May 1947, in a strong easterly gale, the Canadian steamship *Port Royal Park*, of 7,131 gross tons, crashed broadside into Penarth pier. She was unladen and bound from Newport to Cardiff to take on a cargo for the Persian Gulf. Apart from a coastguard who was on watch in the lookout on the jetty and several fishermen, only a few people had braved the weather to take a stroll on the pier. They ran to the promenade for safety as they saw the ship being driven inexorably towards them and that a crash was inevitable. A dance had just started in the Marina Ballroom, at the shore end of the pier, but the building was quickly evacuated. The *Port Royal Park* came to rest with her bows within fifty yards of the promenade and eye witnesses described how the ship seemed to 'lean' on the pier, which cracked under the strain. Much of the planking had been broken or splintered and the metal work had been badly twisted.

The steamer was towed clear when the gale had moderated on the following day; she had sustained little more than superficial damage. The pier, however, had taken the full impact of the collision, and the extensive damage necessitated repairs which were to take it out of commission to both promenaders and steamers for just over two years.

Piers were causing problems on the south coast as well as in the Bristol Channel. Because of war-time neglect most of them were in a poor state of repair, and some had been 'gapped', whereby entire sections had been removed as an anti-invasion measure. As early as March 1946 a Brighton newspaper reported 'Piers may re-open at Easter'. However, it was not until 1947 that the *Glen Gower* was to resume the White Funnel Fleet's south coast sailings.

The *Glen Gower's* war service had taken serious toll and her extensive refit had included the renewal of most of her promenade decking and the construction of a new bridge. The Ministry of War Transport's senior surveyor strongly recommended that stability tests should be carried out as their experience with similar vessels had shown that on reconditioning after war service, stability was frequently less favourable than pre-war. The tests were carried out on Monday 12 May and the results proved to be satisfactory.

FIRST POST-WAR TRIP.—The paddle steamer Glen Gower leaving the Palace Pier Brighton, yesterday. Her passengers for this first trip since the war were the conference delegates of the Institute of Park Administration. Inset, the Captain, E. A. C. Phillips, D.S.C.

White Funnels return to Brighton! A newspaper photograph of the Glen Gower *leaving Palace Pier on the first post-war trip, Wednesday 21 May 1947.*

The *Glen Gower* left Cardiff at 09.14 on Saturday 17 May 1947 under the command of Capt. E.C. Phillips. She arrived at Newhaven at 17.25 on the following day; a journey of just over thirty-two hours duration which included about forty-five minutes circling off Barry for the calibration of her Radio Direction Finder, and steaming at slow speed because of fog off both Land's End and Start Point. The first post-war trip, which took place on the afternoon of Wednesday 21 May 1947, was a return sailing from Brighton to Ryde.

Meanwhile, in the Bristol Channel, further problems had been encountered by the *Glen Usk*. Her log book entry for Wednesday 7 May 1947 states:

> *20.35 Berthing at Weston pier, tide down hard on pier, centre of starboard sponson contacted No. 4 pile, ship had slight headway. Following damage sustained – Spring beam fractured, star centre out of alignment. All possible precautions were taken in approaching pier.*

The 'Spring beam' is a baulk of timber, with a cross section of about 15ins x 12ins which is positioned athwartships at the after end of the paddle box. The material used is usually American Rock Elm or, sometimes Greenheart, from South America, a particularly hard wood, greatly resistant to salt water and one of the few timbers which does not float. Its function is to act as a 'shock-absorber' when berthing. However, a severe blow will cause it to fracture.

The 'star centre' is an integral part of the paddle wheel's feathering mechanism. For a paddle to function at maximum efficiency the floats should enter and leave the water at such an angle that, while immersed, they give the greatest amount of thrust. To achieve this, the angle of each float is adjusted, as the paddle revolves, by the radius rod attached to it. Each radius rod is attached, in turn, to the star centre, a circular disc which rotates around a spindle mounted on the inside of the paddle box, offset from the central axis of the wheel. The star centre is sometimes referred to as the 'Jenny Nettle', or by the slang term 'the Banjo'.

Despite the damage to the *Glen Usk's* spring beam and star centre she was able to proceed to Cardiff and was in service on the following day but on Friday 9 May 1947 she entered the Queen Alexandra Dock, Cardiff, where the Mountstuart Ship Repairing Co. began the necessary repairs. The *Ravenwood's* temporary retirement was cut short when she came out to replace her. The *Glen Usk* re-entered service on Sunday 18 May but, next day, had the misfortune to experience an almost identical accident:

> *21.05 Weston. Tide ebbing 3 to 4 knots on pier. Ship fell down heavily on starboard sponson damaging spring beam and star centre, other damage unknown.*

This time the problem was much more serious and the ship lay immobile at the pier. As the tide ebbed, arrangements were made for towage; the log continues:

> Tuesday 20 May 1947
>
> *00.20 Ship grounded at Weston pier.*
> *Stern off and lying on even keel, comfortable on mud and shingle, fine weather. No apparent straining.*
> *04.20 Floated and re-berthed. Damage to bottom, if any, unknown.*

06.50 Tugs alongside
06.59 Left pier in tow with tugs, The Rose *and* Archibald Hood
08.22 Anchored in Walton Bay.
18.30 Pilot boarded forward tug, The Rose.
20.00 Entered river.
21.03 Entered Cumberland Basin.
21.45 Moored up.

The subsequent repairs took three days and she was in service again for the Whitsun weekend commencing on Saturday 24 May 1947 with a day trip from Cardiff to Ilfracombe.

The *Ravenswood* was then in trouble on Monday 9 June 1947. She left Newport at 10.00 and Weston at 11.40 for a cruise towards the Flat and Steep Holms. while approaching Weston on the return she came to an abrupt halt with 'broken radius rods'. At 12.45 she dropped anchor off the Honeycombe buoy and sent a wireless message to the office at Bristol, via the Burnham Radio station, reporting her plight. The message was unanswered; it was repeated at 13.09, again with no reply. At 13.25 the message was radioed to the *Glen Usk*, then landing her passengers at Weston pier, requesting towage, which was acknowledged immediately. The log books of the two steamers record:

Glen Usk
13.26 Left Pier.
13.36 Whilst approaching Ravenswood *in order to pass tow rope aboard, we damaged our for'd port sponson and paddle box, through ebb tide setting us down on* Ravenswood's *for'd sponson. Weather conditions – strong westerly breeze, high confused sea.* Ravenswood *lying athwart wind and tide, listed to starboard, rolling heavily. Her forward sponson came down on our for'd sponson.* Ravenswood's *tow rope (6in) was made fast and she commenced heaving up.*
13.50 Strain in tow rope. Anchor aweigh and proceeded towards Cardiff Roads.
14.33 Weston buoy abeam.
15.04 West Cardiff buoy abeam.

Ravenswood
15.26 Port anchor down, Middle Pool, Cardiff Roads. Glen Usk *slipped tow.*

Glen Usk
15.32 Proceeded alongside Ravenswood *to disembark passengers but owing to strong ebb tide and wind, decided to wait until slack water.*
15.40 Anchored close to Middle Cardiff buoy.
17.13 Hove up.
17.20 Anchor aweigh and proceeded alongside Ravenswood.
17.40 Alongside. Proceeded embarking passengers.
17.46 Passengers on board and proceeded towards Weston.
19.00 Off Weston, awaiting signal to come alongside.
19.15 Alongside and disembarked passengers.

The *Glen Usk* then continued with her day's work. Just after 21.00 the *Ravenswood* was taken in tow by two local tugs and by 21.45 was all fast at the Pier Head, Cardiff. Repairs were effected to her starboard paddle wheel over the next few days and she was back in service on Friday 13 June 1947.

The second, new paddle steamer of the post-war era had been launched on Wednesday 26 February 1947 by Mrs Banks, wife of the Managing Director, at Fairfield's yard, Govan, Glasgow. She had been named *Cardiff Queen* and by the beginning of June 1947 her fitting out was nearing completion. Her log book opens on Thursday 12 June 1947 when, under the command of Capt. Lachlan McLean Shedden, she ran her acceptance trials in the Firth of Clyde.

Unlike the *Bristol Queen,* she ran official Board of Trade trials and made a total of eight runs on the measured mile; the two best being:

Down 16.942 knots, at 51.65 r.p.m.
Up 17.145 knots, at 52.70 r.p.m.

These are the figures recorded by Fairfield's representatives and show a mean speed of 17.04 knots – below the guaranteed speed of eighteen knots. She returned to Fairfield's basin at Govan for engine adjustments and left there again on Monday 16 June 1947 to run a further, unofficial trial on the Skelmorlie measured mile during which the following figures were recorded:

The second new paddle steamer of the post-war era slides into the murky waters of the River Clyde on Wednesday 26 February 1947. The Cardiff Queen *was launched at Fairfield's yard, Govan by Mrs W.J. Banks, the wife of P&A Campbell's managing director.* (Graham E. Langmuir)

The Cardiff Queen *at Fairfield's fitting out berth in March 1947.* (Graham E. Langmuir)

The Cardiff Queen *running trials on the Skelmorlie measured mile in the Firth of Clyde, Thursday 12 June 1947.* (Chris Collard Collection)

Down Two runs, 16.605 knots.
Up Two runs, 18.442 knots.
Mean speed, 17.5 knots.

She was still half a knot slower than her specified speed.

After these trials she anchored in Gourock Bay for further engine adjustments until 22.30 that night, when she sailed for Bristol:

Monday 16 June 1947
22.30 Dep. Gourock.
22.40 Cloch Lt. abeam. Course S.W. Log set.
23.02 Skelmorlie buoy. Log 5.3.
23.43 Cumbrae Lt. Log 13.6.
Day ends. Wind S, 3-4. O'cast. Showery. Moderate sea.

Tuesday 17 June 1947
Day opens. Wind S, 3-4, Increasing. Mod – rough sea.
00.42 Holy Isle, Arran, abeam.
01.55 Ailsa Craig.
03.00 Corsewall Point. Log 56.5.
04.08 Black Head.
05.00 Mew Island. Log 79.
06.30 Sea bent forward stanchions and broke teak rail.
Tiles lifting from floors in forward lavatories.
09.40 Calf of Man.

Between the Isle of Man and the North Wales coast the weather deteriorated to such an extent that the *Cardiff Queen* was forced to run for shelter. At 14.30 off Point Lynas, Anglesey, a pilot was boarded who took her into Holyhead harbour where, two hours later, she was moored at the Town Berth. She sheltered in Holyhead overnight and by noon on the following day conditions had moderated sufficiently for her to proceed. She sailed at 12.15, arrived at Fishguard at 18.15 where she took on fuel, and sailed again at 20.30. At 01.50 on Thursday 19 June she passed the St. Gowans Lightvessel; at 03.15, the Helwick Lightvessel; the Scarweather Lightvessel at 04.20 and the Breaksea Lightvessel at 06.45. She entered the River Avon at 07.50, passed the *Bristol Queen* at Hotwells Landing Stage and entered the Cumberland basin at 08.30, after a journey of 430 miles from Gourock.

Later that morning she was moored at the Underfall Yard for repairs to her forward rail and final preparations for entering service. It was found that she left much to be desired; as well as rust already showing on her hull, some of her boiler tubes were leaking, paddle arm bushes were worn, deckheads were leaking and a variety of other imperfections were apparent on inspection.

The *Cardiff Queen* began her season on Saturday 21 June 1947, on the Cardiff to Weston ferry. Her first trip down channel was on Sunday 22 June – a day trip to Ilfracombe with a cruise to Lundy Roads. Thereafter she spent most of the season on the Cardiff to Ilfracombe

The Cardiff Queen *arriving at Bristol from the Clyde on the morning of Thursday 19 June 1947. On her way south, heavy seas bent the forward, starboard stanchions, causing the teak rail to break. The forward sections of the canvas weathercloths were then removed from her bows in order to prevent further damage, and remained absent for the whole of her first season.* (Ernest Dumbleton)

The Cardiff Queen *receives attention at the Underfall yard on Thursday 19 June 1947, before entering service two days later.* (Edwin Keen)

service, sometimes changing places with the *Bristol Queen* on the Bristol to Ilfracombe route, and making very occasional calls at Newport and Swansea.

During her first season the *Cardiff Queen* displayed a number of unusual features by way of appearance. The canvas dodger around her foredeck extended only about three quarters of the way along her forward rails and she carried another canvas dodger which extended right around her after deck. Her name pennant, instead of the usual dark blue with white lettering, was white with red lettering and she carried a jack-staff at both her bow and stern. All of these features, along with the pale salmon saloon strake being painted narrower than in subsequent years, were present in 1947 only. It should also be mentioned that the *Cardiff Queen* originally carried two bells, one on the foremast and another on the mainmast. One had been inherited from the *Westward Ho*, her name having been ground out and that of the *Cardiff Queen* engraved in its place. Other items which she inherited from the *Westward Ho* were the bronze staircase leading from the after sun lounge to the main deck abaft the engine room, bridge telegraphs, brass porthole surrounds and her brass chime whistle.

June 1947 also saw the long awaited arrival of the turbine steamer *Empress Queen*. With her refit complete, Capt. Jack George, his officers and crew took her over on Tuesday 17 June 1947 and sailed from the Ailsa Shipbuilding Co.'s yard at Troon at 17.00 for Bristol. She made a good passage south, missing the worst of the bad weather which had delayed the *Cardiff Queen*.

On the evening of Wednesday 18 June 1947, over seven years after being launched, she made her way up the River Avon, with the assistance of two tugs, into the Cumberland Basin. On the morning of Monday 23 June she was towed to Narrow Quay, at the City Centre and that afternoon was open for inspection by the Directors and Shareholders of the company. The ship had been the 'brain child' of the Managing Director, Mr W.J. Banks. He had served the company for fifty years and his retirement coincided with the arrival of the turbine steamer. To mark the occasion a reception and presentation were held aboard on that afternoon. On the following day she was open to the public in aid of the Royal National Lifeboat Institution.

The *Empress Queen* was an outstandingly beautiful vessel of 1,781.25 gross tons, fitted with turbines by Harland & Wolff of Belfast, with a single, double ended, oil fired boiler giving her a service speed of about 17.5 knots. She could carry up to 1,300 passengers and her well appointed accommodation consisted of two passenger decks, an after dining saloon to seat 108 people, a forward dining saloon to seat forty, a sun lounge, bar and cocktail bar.

She was originally destined for the south coast, primarily to operate the cross channel day trips, but after the war Government restrictions effectively suspended such excursions and alternative employment had to be considered for her. Her size precluded her sailing in the upper reaches of the Bristol Channel so it was decided that she should take over the lucrative Swansea to Ilfracombe service.

Her season began on Friday 27 June 1947 when she left Bristol for Swansea, assisted through the docks and down the river by the tugs *John King* and *Volunteer*. They cast off at the mouth of the river at 16.15 and she took the passage inside the Nash Sands arriving at Swansea at 19.47. She turned outside the breakwater and made her way up the river Tawe to Pockett's Wharf, stern first, using her bow rudder to manoeuvre. At 20.00 she left on her first

Aboard the Empress Queen, *open to the public, on Tuesday 24 June 1947. A boarding charge of sixpence per person was made in aid of the Royal National Lifeboat Institution.* (Edwin Keen)

civilian passenger sailing – a cruise around the Scarweather Lightvessel – dressed overall and carrying about 300 passengers. On the following day she began what was to become the daily service to Ilfracombe, but this was curtailed on Tuesday 1 July 1947 when she struck the pier face at Ilfracombe with some force, while coming in after lying in the Range – the anchorage half a mile offshore.

She sustained damage to her stem, hawse pipe and bulwarks which necessitated her entering the Prince of Wales Dock, Swansea, on the following morning for repairs. These were completed by Saturday 5 July 1947 when she left the dock early in the morning to run a day return trip from Briton Ferry to llfracombe, on charter to the Briton Ferry Workingmen's Club and Institute. A further day trip to Ilfracombe and an evening cruise to off Porthcawl took place on Sunday 6 July 1947 which, after only seven days in service, were her last Bristol Channel sailings.

Her period at Swansea had not been a success, having damaged herself at both Ilfracombe, and at Briton Ferry on her morning call of the previous day, when she bumped the jetty with some force and dented her hull. Capt. George was the most experienced Bristol Channel master and was well used to handling the ship, having been her commander during the war. However, despite the advantages of a bow rudder, the combination of her size and propulsion meant that she lacked the manoeuvrability of the paddle steamers, so essential in the narrow confines of some of the Bristol Channel ports of call. It was announced, therefore, that all sailings from Swansea would be cancelled

The Empress Queen *passing Hotwells Landing Stage on her way to take up her station at Swansea, Friday 27 June 1947.* (Cyril Hawkins Garrington)

Having cast off her two tugs at the mouth of the River Avon, the Empress Queen *reaches full speed as she passes Battery Point, Portishead, on her way down channel, Friday 27 June 1947.* (Edwin Keen)

The Empress Queen *leaving Swansea. June/July 1947.* (H.G. Owen Collection)

until further notice from Monday 7 July and the decision was made to interchange her with the *Glen Gower* at Brighton.

The *Empress Queen* left Swansea for the south coast on the evening of Monday 7 July 1947 and headed across the channel into a strong westerly wind, rough sea and heavy swell. At 22.35 she was abeam of the South Lundy Lighthouse and by midnight she was encountering squalls of gale force, labouring heavily and shipping water forward. Capt. George's log book entry for Tuesday 8 July 1947 states:

> *01.20 Trevose Head bearing S.E. Distance 10 miles*
> *Put about for Lundy Isle.*
> *04.30 In lee of Lundy.*
> *09.15 Shifted anchorage towards Lundy for more lee*
> *09.45 Brought up port cable 3 shackles*
> *Forward bulwarks inspected and found to be bent overnight by heavy seas.*

She remained in the shelter of Lundy until 08.30 on the following day when, with the wind moderating, she hove up and proceeded. At 15.05 she passed the Longships Lighthouse and arrived at Newhaven at 07.00 on Thursday 10 July 1947. On the next day she ran a trial trip without passengers from Newhaven and Brighton to Ryde, returning direct to Newhaven, and began her south coast season on Saturday 12 July 1947. On the same day the *Glen Gower*, now under the command of Capt. W. Riddell, left Newhaven

The Empress Queen *at Newhaven on Thursday 10 July 1947, shortly after her arrival from the Bristol Channel.* (Chris Collard Collection)

The Empress Queen *arriving at Palace Pier, Brighton, in 1947.* (Chris Collard Collection)

and returned to the Bristol Channel, where she re-opened the Swansea to Ilfracombe service on Tuesday 15 July 1947. She made the first post war sailing from Porthcawl on Wednesday 27 August with an afternoon cruise to off St. Donats Castle, just to the east of Nash Point.

The *Glen Usk* was in trouble once again when, on the afternoon of Tuesday 22 July 1947 on a crossing from Weston to Cardiff, her Chief Engineer, John Taylor, discovered that the engine room bilges were full of water. Her next departure from Cardiff was delayed until the water was under control. She proceeded to Weston and then to Barry where, despite the pumps working on the bilges, the water was found to be gaining slightly. Her channel cruise from Barry was cancelled while the Chief Engineer traced the source of the leak – a crack in the garboard strake plate on the port side close to the engine room after bulkhead – which had now developed into a hole. The Chief Engineer placed a sack with red lead putty into the hole, which reduced the inflow of water to an amount within the capabilities of the pumps. All further sailings for the day were cancelled and she made her way direct to the Pier Head, Cardiff, where the company's Marine Superintendent, Mr John MacGregor, was waiting with workmen from the Mountstuart Dry Dock. Temporary repairs were completed by the early hours of the following morning; no further problems were encountered in this respect and permanent repairs were effected during the following winter.

On the afternoon of Sunday 27 July the *Cardiff Queen,* on a cruise from Bristol to the English & Welsh Grounds Lightvessel, ran on to the mud on the Gloucestershire bank of the most dangerous part of the River Avon, the notorious Horseshoe bend. Fortunately the tide was on the flood and she soon refloated, continuing the cruise apparently undamaged. She ran her last trips of the season on Tuesday 23 September and berthed alongside the *Glen Gower* at the Underfall Yard on the following day, looking very much the worse for wear, with her hull and funnels badly rusted. Throughout the season she had been plagued by boiler and paddle troubles which caused the cancellation of the equivalent of at least a week's sailings. In addition there were continuing deck head leaks, the flooring in the saloons cracked open, and the main condensor seating was not properly finished. Numerous other faults were apparent and Fairfield's engineers were called in during the winter. Many of the defects were remedied but she was never an entirely satisfactory vessel. In a letter of complaint to Fairfield's as late as 13 August 1952 the Managing Director stated, among other things, 'In general the vessel has not reached our expectations as a Clyde-built steamer.'

In contrast, the *Bristol Queen* had a relatively trouble free season mechanically, with only one day's sailings lost, owing to engine repairs, on Thursday 26 June 1947. Ten days earlier, representatives of the National Physical Laboratory, Teddington, had been aboard. She was delayed at Barry, en route from Bristol to Ilfracombe while their apparatus was rigged. The log book states 'Speed experiments by Nat. Lab. Officials.' Neither the exact nature of the experiments, nor the results are recorded but undoubtedly they were testing the efficiency of the hull, in the design of which they had played a large part.

The *Glen Gower* had experienced a somewhat difficult season, over a week's sailings having been lost because of boiler trouble. On 30 May 1947, only nine days after entering service, P&A Campbell Ltd wrote to the Ministry of War Transport:

> *The boiler of this vessel was surveyed with the greatest care both at the beginning and towards the end of her reconditioning and defects made good.*
>
> *Despite this, since going into service, we have experienced great trouble with her boiler tubes; the vessel having been laid off on two occasions within a week, with a consequent loss of revenue. Already we have had to deal with over 200 tubes, some of which were pitted externally. The constant expanding of these tubes is now beginning to make them too thin, and no estimate can be made of how long the vessel will continue in service.*

The letter continued by stating that at the Admiralty's survey prior to her war service the condition of the boiler was found to be good, and ended with the submission:

> *We are of the opinion that its defective condition is due to treatment during her war service. In these circumstances, we feel strongly that it is fair and reasonable that this boiler should be re-tubed at the expense of the Ministry.*

The Ministry's representatives accordingly carried out an inspection of the boiler while the vessel was off service at Newhaven. Negotiations then followed which culminated in the Ministry's sanctioning the replacement of the defective tubes during the following winter.

Another problem experienced, not only with the *Glen Gower* but with the other coal-burning steamers, *Glen Usk* and *Ravenswood*, was that of poor firing.

Efficient firing depended on the required steam pressure being produced at all times, not always an easy task. A day's sailings would begin, perhaps, in the morning with a run at half

The Glen Gower *re-opening the Swansea service, after the withdrawal of the* Empress Queen, *with a day trip to Ilfracombe on Tuesday 15 July 1947.* (H.G. Owen)

The Cardiff Queen *off Ilfracombe on Sunday 20 July 1947. She had arrived on a day trip from Cardiff and Weston at 14.15 and anchored close to the pier, (from where this photograph was taken), owing to the increasingly fresh south-easterly wind. Capt. Shedden is on the bridge, and on the foredeck two seamen have just started the donkey engine to raise the anchor, prior to her berthing at the pier for her 18.00 departure.* (H.G. Owen)

The Cardiff Queen *turning in the River Tawe on Saturday 13 September 1947. She had been sent to Swansea that morning to take two of the* Glen Gower's *crossings to Ilfracombe, while the latter was undergoing boiler repairs.* (H.G. Owen)

speed down river. Then out to sea, with a series of calls at various piers with short runs at full speed in between. Next a long run at full speed followed by a final call and a few hours at anchor before a similar return journey. Throughout the day the firemen would be watching the pressure gauge, ensuring that an adequate supply of steam was available for each varying stage of the journey, no more nor less than the engines demanded.

With more and more ships being oil fired, efficient firemen were becoming a dying breed. Fewer and fewer men were willing to spend their days shovelling coal in a dark, hot, lurching stokehold, and fewer of those who were possessed the requisite skill and stamina for the job.

Consideration had been given to the conversion of the *Glen Gower* to oil firing as early as 1936, when the Wallsend Slipway & Engineering Co. Ltd had been asked for a quotation for the work. Similar estimates had been called for in October 1945 for both the *Glen Gower* and *Glen Usk*, and another was requested for the *Glen Gower* in October 1947. Yet another was to be asked for in September 1949 but such conversions never took place.

To return to 1947; on the south coast the *Empress Queen*, in comparison with her troublesome ten days in the Bristol Channel, had a relatively uneventful season. Her restricted manoeuvrability was once again a drawback, making her slow at berthing at the piers and causing a few bumps and scrapes. Mechanical problems were prevalent especially in the first few weeks but there was little disruption to sailings.

However, her first visit to Southampton on Friday 15 July 1947 was marred by a three-hour delay at anchor off Netley because of engine trouble on the return trip to Brighton.

She was instrumental in a rescue on Monday 25 August 1947. At 04.00, while at anchor off Brighton, the night watchman heard cries for help and discovered two men adrift in an open boat. Immediately Capt. George ordered the lowering of one of the motor lifeboats which picked up the men and brought them safely on board, landing them at Brighton later that morning.

Her season ended on Sunday 14 September 1947 with a day trip from Brighton to Ryde, and she arrived at Bristol on Tuesday 16 September 1947 after a somewhat rough, but uneventful round trip. The ports and resorts re-opened on the south coast during 1947 were Newhaven, Brighton – both Palace Pier and West Pier, Hastings, Ryde, Bournemouth and Southampton. All initial calls were made by the *Glen Gower* and all were subsequently visited by the *Empress Queen*.

The *Britannia* remained out of commission at Bristol for the whole of the 1947 season. Negotiations with the Admiralty had been completed and they agreed to pay £24,000 towards the cost of her replacement boiler; this figure is believed to have been 95% of its total cost. The company ordered, on Mr Banks's advice, a large, double-ended, oil fired Scotch boiler to be made by Fairfield's of Govan, which was transported south by road at the end of June.

The defunct, haystack boiler having been removed, and modifications to the boiler room having been made, the *Britannia* left Bristol at 04.00 on Tuesday 1 July for Cardiff, where the new boiler was to be lifted into position by the floating crane, none of the cranes at Bristol or Avonmouth being able to handle it. She was taken in tow by the tugs *Eastleigh* and *John King*, (also the *Volunteer* in the River Avon), and arrived in the Roath Dock at about mid-

The Britannia *in the Roath Dock, Cardiff, on Tuesday 1 July 1947. Her new boiler has been temporarily lifted out while a number of modifications are being made to the boiler room.* (Leslie Hansen)

day. The crane had been ordered for 12.30 but when the boiler was lowered into the hull it became apparent that further modifications were needed to the boiler room. The boiler was therefore removed while the necessary work was carried out, and was successfully positioned about an hour later. The tugs then towed her back to Bristol where she was moored at Charles Hill's yard at 21.30 that evening.

It was then necessary for the Board of Trade to carry out stability tests, the ship's metacentric height having become lowered. She failed the tests, making further modifications necessary, which this time were more drastic. They entailed the removal of her after deck house, the moving forward of the bridge, and the removal of her two forward lifeboats, one of which was destined to become the *Lynmouth Queen,* one of the motor launches used to land passengers at Lynmouth from 1949 onwards. As a consequence of the alterations, her No 2 certificate had to be surrendered and her No.3 certificate restricted her to carrying a maximum of 800 passengers, nearly 100 less that previously allowed.

A rectangular, steel chequer plate was fitted to the deck above the boiler room which, owing to the close proximity of the boiler to the deckhead, became very hot. Additionally, in later years, a guard-rail, a few feet high, was positioned around the forward end of each funnel with a notice affixed warning passengers of the considerable heat which could be generated. The reboilering and subsequent modifications meant that she would not re-enter service until the 1948 season.

After the 'Big Freeze' at the beginning of the year came an exceptionally fine summer with long spells of dry weather. Consequently, passenger figures were high and the company's trading profit for the 1947 season was a very healthy £106,181.

Ilfracombe in the summer of 1947 with the Cardiff Queen *at the Stone Bench.* (Chris Collard Collection)

1948/1949 – Seven Steamers

1948 was the year in which the White Funnel Fleet reached its full post war strength with all six paddle steamers and the *Empress Queen* in service.

The *Glen Usk* with Capt. Findlay Brander in command, opened the season on Thursday 25 March 1948, just before Easter, and spent most of her time on the Cardiff to Weston ferry. The *Ravenswood*, with Capt. L. McL. Shedden, and *Glen Gower*, with Capt. Albert V. Murphy, began service in mid-May; the former helping out on the Cardiff to Weston route as well as maintaining the Newport sailings, and the latter supporting both the *Ravenswood* and *Glen Usk* up channel, taking most of the Bristol – Cardiff – Ilfracombe trips until mid-June.

The *Britannia* left Bristol on trials on Monday 10 May, looking resplendent after her refit with two funnels. Her new boiler peformed well and for the first time in her career she was based on the south coast for the whole of the season. It was necessary for her to refuel on her round trips and she put into Falmouth for that purpose on each occasion. On Wednesday 12 May 1948, under the command of Capt. E.C. Phillips, she left the Cumberland Basin at 09.20, passed Hartland Point at 15.00, Lands End at 20.22 and anchored off Falmouth at 23.15. After refuelling in Falmouth Harbour on the following morning she left at 11.40 and after a delay because of fog off the Isle of Wight, arrived at Newhaven at 03.40 on Friday 14 May 1948. Her first trips took place on the following day and included the first post-war sailing from the newly re-opened Eastbourne pier. She also resumed post-war sailings from Shanklin on Tuesday 8 June 1948.

The *Cardiff Queen* appeared on Saturday 12 June 1948, under the command of Capt. J.A. Harris, and promptly disgraced herself by running into the mud at the Horseshoe Bend, River Avon, on her way down channel from Bristol. The dipping edge of one of her starboard paddle floats was bent but no other damage was apparent and she continued her sailings with little delay.

The Britannia, *with her new boiler successfully installed, two funnels fitted and other modifications complete, receives a good coating of anti-rust paint at Bristol. Saturday 27 March 1948.* (Edwin Keen)

Steam being raised from the Britannia's *new boiler on Sunday 9 May 1948.* (Edwin Keen)

The Britannia *returning from boiler trials on Monday 10 May 1948.* (Edwin Keen)

The Ravenswood *in the Cumberland Basin early in the 1948 season.* (Chris Collard Collection)

The *Bristol Queen* entered service on Saturday 19 June with Capt. Jack George in command, thus allowing the *Glen Gower* to commence the Swansea sailings.

A number of unusual charter trips took place towards the end of June 1948. On Thursday 24 June the *Glen Gower* ran a day trip to Weston from Port Talbot, negotiating the berth at the dock entrance with the assistance of a tug.

On Saturday 26 June the Briton Ferry Workingmen's Club and Institute chartered both the *Glen Gower* and *Ravenswood* for a day trip to Weston.

The appearance of the *Ravenswood* so far down channel was unique; Nash Point being the western limit of her sailings along the Welsh coast in the post-war years. She completed her ferry sailings on Friday 25 June and left Cardiff for Briton Ferry, after coaling, at 23.00. At midnight, off the Breaksea Light Vessel, she encountered fog and rough seas but at 02.00 on Saturday 26 June she passed the Scarweather Lightvessel and at 02.50 dropped anchor in Swansea Bay. Later that morning she berthed at Briton Ferry, embarked her passengers and left at 08.15, about half an hour before the departure of the *Glen Gower*, which had recently arrived from Swansea. The *Ravenswood* arrived at Weston at 12.50, about an hour after the arrival of the *Glen Gower*. Both steamers then anchored offshore. On the return journey the *Ravenswood* left Weston at 18.05 followed by the *Glen Gower* at 19.00, arriving at Briton Ferry at 23.15 and 22.57 respectively. The *Glen Gower* then returned to Swansea and the *Ravenswood* returned up channel. The latter left Briton Ferry at 00.13 on Sunday 27 June 1948 and after a rough passage arrived at Barry at 04.25. She then left Barry at 08.05 and arrived at Newport in time to start her day's sailings at 10.15.

The *Bristol Queen*, with the assistance of the tug, *John King*, was moored at the Narrow Quay, City Centre, Bristol, on Monday 28 June in readiness for a charter, two days later, in connection with the celebrations of 100 years municipal ownership of the Bristol City Docks. The Lord Mayor, City Councillors and guests boarded her on the morning of Wednesday 30 June for a trip through the Floating Harbour, again with the assistance of the *John King*, and then down the river to Avonmouth, where the party disembarked in the locks for lunch and an inspection of the port.

On the south coast the *Britannia* was running well until a number of leaking rivets were discovered in her hull, near the engine room, which necessitated her going on to the gridiron in Newhaven Harbour for repairs on Monday 5 July; she was back in service on the following day.

The tug John King *towing the* Bristol Queen *down St. Augustines Reach in the Bristol City Docks on Wednesday 30 June 1948. The steamer was chartered by the Port of Bristol Authority in connection with the celebrations of 100 years municipal ownership of the docks.* (Chris Collard Collection)

Her consort at Brighton during that season was the *Empress Queen* under the command of Capt. William A. Couves, the former master of the pre-war *Brighton Queen*. She left Bristol at 07.30 on Wednesday 7 July 1948, her passage down the Avon assisted, as usual, by two tugs. After compass adjusting off Barry she passed the Breaksea Lightvessel at 11.05, Hartland Point at 15.15 and the Longships Lighthouse at 20.50. On the following morning she was abeam of

The Empress Queen *on the gridiron in Newhaven harbour. The* Britannia *is tucked into her berth on the left, Friday 9 July 1948.* (Chris Collard Collection)

the Eddystone Lighthouse at 01.05 and arrived off Newhaven at 13.15; the log book records her average speed for the journey as 15.15 knots. She went on to the gridiron on Friday 9 July for bottom painting and began her eight week season on Saturday 10 July 1948.

The Bristol Channel sailings proceeded satisfactorily apart from two incidents involving the *Cardiff Queen*. She left Hotwells Landing Stage at 22.55 on Tuesday 27 July to return to Cardiff when, just above Sea Mills, a tug with barges in tow collided with her. She hit the mud bank with her starboard paddle, damaging a float and the rim. This was the paddle which she had already damaged on her first day in service but, as on that occasion, she was able to proceed on her journey after only a slight delay.

On Saturday 4 September she was on one of her usual Cardiff – Barry – Ilfracombe sailings. She left Barry at 12.22 and arrived off Ilfracombe at about 15.00 in very rough seas and a strong northerly wind which prevented her from entering the harbour. Capt. Harris hove to for about two and a half hours, steaming about ten miles, before the weather had moderated sufficiently for her to berth.

The season otherwise continued uneventfully and reached its close on Monday 11 October 1948. Although the ships ran well it had been a season of variable weather, which adversely affected the passenger figures and resulted in a trading profit of £36,966, less than a third of that of the previous season.

During 1949 the deployment of the steamers and pattern of sailings were virtually the same as in 1948. The *Glen Usk* with Capt. Brander in command, opened the season on Wednesday 13 April

The Cardiff Queen *arriving at Newport on the evening of Thursday 24 June 1948 after a charter trip to Ilfracombe by the Charles Lyne Lodge of Freemasons. She is turning on a flood tide; a fascinating manoeuvre whereby her stem is about to be run a few feet into the mud of the east bank. With her bow held fast the flow of the tide will swing her stern around. She will then back off and drift upstream until adjacent to the landing stage, where, with careful use of the engines, she will be brought alongside.* (John Brown)

The Glen Gower *arrives and departs from Swansea on a Saturday evening in 1948.* (H.G. Owen)

1949, just before Easter, and all other paddle steamers were in service by Whit-Sunday June 5.

A criticism of the *Bristol Queen* since her entry into service was that her two after lifeboats took up too much space on the promenade deck and obscured the passengers view. When she appeared at the start of the 1949 season, with Capt. Jack George again in command, the lifeboats had been raised and were supported on platforms half way up the davits, which pleased the passengers, but not the helmsmen. The lifeboats acted as a kind of sail and added considerably to the wind resistance of the after part of the ship, making her even more difficult to handle in cross winds.

The *Britannia* began her south coast sailings, with Capt. E.C. Phillips in command, on Whit-Sunday 5 June 1949 and had the distinction of making the first post war calls at the piers of Worthing, on the following day, and Bognor Regis on Tuesday 7 June. Her consort, the *Empress Queen*, again under the Command of Capt. W.A. Couves, began her season at the beginning of July.

Several ports of call were re-opened in the Bristol Channel. Penarth pier had been repaired and calls were resumed by the *Glen Usk* on Saturday 4 June 1949. Regular motor boat landings were re-commenced from the *Cardiff Queen*, with Capt. J.A. Harris in command, at Lynmouth on Whit-Monday 6 June and from the *Glen Gower*, with Capt A.V. Murphy, at Lundy on Monday 20 June.

Two unusual incidents were experienced by the *Glen Usk* in July. On Wednesday 13, while weighing anchor off Weston, the Cardiff pleasure launch *Perfaith* was seen, apparently in diffi-

The Bristol Queen *leaving Bristol on her first trip of the season – an afternoon sailing to Clevedon, Cardiff and Barry – on Saturday 4 June 1949. Her two after lifeboats have now been raised from deck level.* (Edwin Keen)

Captain Findlay Brander brings the Glen Usk *alongside Birnbeck Pier, Weston, in 1949. On a calm day and with a slack tide, berthing was relatively easy. However, adverse weather conditions and strong tides made it one of the country's most difficult landing places. For some years a brewery advertisement was situated at the end of the jetty, facing seaward. The irony of its message was, no doubt, lost on the brewery, but not on the ships' officers – it read 'Weston – Take Courage'.* (Seaton Phillips)

culties, off Swallow Point. After embarking her passengers and leaving Birnbeck Pier the *Glen Usk* steamed to the *Perfaith* and took her in tow. The weather at the time could hardly have been worse – 'Gale force NW wind, heavy seas, heavy rain squalls. Thunder and lightning, visibility poor.' However, both vessels arrived safely at Cardiff at 19.02.

On Monday 25 July she went to investigate another cabin cruiser, again off Swallow Point. The vessel was adrift, with no one aboard. The *Glen Usk* proceeded on her way, notifying the Burnham Radio Station who arranged for the Weston lifeboat to recover the abandoned motor boat.

On the evening of Friday 22 July, the *Bristol Queen*, on her return from Ilfracombe to Barry, Weston and Cardiff, dropped anchor six miles west of the Breaksea Lightvessel; a driving arm in the port paddle had broken. The *Ravenswood* left Cardiff at 20.55 to go to her assistance and towed her to Barry. The *Bristol Queen's* Cardiff passengers returned home by train while the sixty-six Weston passengers were transferred to the *Ravenswood* which arrived at Birnbeck Pier at 01.10 on the following day; she then returned light to Cardiff. The *Bristol Queen's* paddle damage was quickly repaired and she was back in service on Saturday 23.

During August 1949 the *Ravenswood* met with crew difficulties. At 20.25 on Monday 8 August, while crossing from Penarth to Weston, a deckhand was working on the forward sponson, contrary to orders, when he was washed overboard, miraculously missing the paddle wheel. The alarm was given for emergency lifeboat stations, Capt. W. F. Watson stopped the ship and ordered a lifeboat to be launched with the Chief Officer, Mr Leslie Brook in charge. The deckhand was picked up at 20.35 none the worse for the experience. Mr Brook's report of the incident ends – 'Put him on to assisting rowing the lifeboat to keep him warm. When on board, rubbed down, given a tot of rum, and to bed.'

Trouble of a more serious nature took place on the *Ravenswood* on Tuesday 30 August when a seaman was given notice and paid off at Newport at the end of her day's sailings. The reason for

The Glen Usk *arriving at Ilfracombe Pier, after lying at anchor offshore, on Thursday 11 August 1949. She is about to take the return sailing to Weston and Newport.* (H.G. Owen)

Captain Albert Murphy brings the Glen Gower *alongside Ilfracombe pier on the afternoon of Thursday 11 August 1949. She had been unable to land her passengers at Lundy owing to the north-westerly wind producing too choppy a sea at the landing beach.* (H.G. Owen)

his dismissal is not known but the entire deck crew, two firemen, three stewards and the deck chair lady immediately gave forty-eight hours notice on account of his leaving. Accordingly, at 22.30 on the evening of Thursday 1 September, they left the ship. The *Ravenswood* was off service at Cardiff on the following day when replacements for all those who had left were signed on.

On Saturday 27 August 1949 the *Cardiff Queen*, under the command of Capt. J.A. Harris, was on her way from Weston to Ilfracombe when, at 13.40, she ran into fog off the North Devon coast and speed had to be reduced. At 14.00 the visibility improved and Lynmouth Foreland was sighted, speed was increased but almost immediately she ran on to the eastern end of the Sandridge Shoal – a sandbank about a mile long running east to west, a mile off Lynmouth. Her engines were put astern but she failed to respond owing to the rapidly falling tide; all of her passengers were then disembarked by the Lynmouth motor launches. The bilges were examined and soundings were taken every fifteen minutes but there was no sign of either bottom damage or strain. She refloated at 16.55 and proceeded to Barry, resuming her advertised sailings for the rest of the day.

It was in 1949 that work commenced on the rebuilding of Ilfracombe Pier. Opened in May 1873, the pier had been the conception of Sir Bourchier Palk Wrey, then Lord of the Manor, whose family owned and maintained it until 1906, when the Ilfracombe Council obtained an Act of Parliament to lease and purchase the pier and harbour undertaking. It had withstood the storms and ravages of time for over seventy years and during 1940 it had been necessary to demolish certain parts of it in accordance with the anti-invasion precautions. This, coupled with deterioration and lack of essential maintenance during war time, had weakened the whole structure. In order that the work might proceed a good deal of underwater construction was necessary and much of this could only be carried out during the two hours or so either side of

RAVENSWOOD

Previous Page: The Ravenswood *arriving at Clevedon on Sunday 26 July 1949.* (Cyril Hawkins Garrington)

low water. The work continued at all times of the day and night by a workforce small in number, never more than twenty five, and was so organised to cause no disruption to the steamer services. It was a major undertaking which was to cost much and which would occupy three years.

The summer of 1949 was exceptionally good and the company's trading profit amounted to £63,814.

The season was closed by the *Glen Usk* on Monday 17 October. In the post war years she was often the first steamer out, the last one in and the one which covered the most mileage. In 1949 the *Empress Queen* steamed 7,507 miles; the *Ravenswood* – 9,205 miles; the *Glen Gower* – 10,063 miles; the *Cardiff Queen* – 11,229 miles; the *Britannia* – 11,954 miles and the *Bristol Queen* – 13,091 miles. The closing entry in the log book of the *Glen Usk* reads:

> *Number of sailing days 190*
> *Number of off service days 24*
> *Number of days cancelled through stress of weather 1*
> *Number of days cancelled for repairs 1*
> *Number of calls at Weston Pier 641*
> *Number of times missed Weston Pier 1*
> *Number of calls at Penarth Pier 518*
> *Total mileage for 1949 season 13,649*

Not a bad season's work!

The Cardiff Queen *at Ilfracombe on Thursday 1 September 1949. The presence of cranes in the background indicates that preliminary work on the reconstruction of the pier is under way.* (H.G. Owen)

1950/1951 – Stormy Weather

At the end of each season the steamers were laid up for the winter in the Floating Harbour at Bristol and outwardly showed little sign of activity until a few weeks into the following year. Preparations then began for the forthcoming season which necessitated a considerable amount of movement of the ships between the company's Underfall Yard, Hill's dry dock and other berths. Incidentally, all of the steamers, including the *Empress Queen*, were able to use Hill's Dry Dock at Bristol except the *Cardiff Queen* and the *Bristol Queen*. The width across their sponsons was too great and before their seasons began they had to make the short journey down the river to Avonmouth for dry docking, sometimes in tow but usually under their own steam. The movements of all the ships were recorded in the memorandum books with details of the personnel involved, boatmen, tugs and cost of towage where necessary; inevitably most of the movements were made with the ships not in steam. A selection of the entries for 1950 are reproduced here to illustrate the activities leading to the opening of the season:

The largest and smallest members of the post-war fleet; the Empress Queen *and the* Ravenswood *in the Merchant's Dock, Bristol, on Sunday 14 May 1950. The overhaul and re-painting of the latter has almost been completed, in readiness for her to begin her season on Friday 26 May.* (Edwin Keen)

Monday 16 January 1950.
Ravenswood. *Capt. W. F. Watson.*
12.00. Ex. dry dock to Merchants Dock.
Two tugs, John King & Volunteer – *£9. One boatman.*
Britannia. *12.15. Ex. dry dock to own yard.*
Two tugs, Roy & Medway – *£9. One boatman.*

Wednesday 15 February 1950.
Empress Queen. *Capt. J A. Kidd.*
06.45. Hill's Dry Dock to Mardyke Wharf.
One tug, Medway – *£5.5.0. One boatman.*

Thursday 2 March 1950.
Bristol Queen. *Capt. J. George.*
09.20. Mardyke Wall to Centre for visit of Princess Elizabeth.
Berthed by 10.00.
Two tugs, Volunteer & John King – *£4.10.0. One boatman.*
Capt. Harris mentions that, while under tow, wind caught BQ broadside causing her to touch S.S. Dagmar Bratt. *Damage, if any, not known.*
Empress Queen. *Capt. J. A. Kidd.*
10.30. Mardyke Wharf to Centre.
Two tugs, Volunteer & John King – *£5. 5. 0. One boatman.*

Monday 20 March 1930.
Empress Queen. *Capt. J.A. Kidd.*
10.30. From Narrow Quay to Merchants Dock.
Two tugs, John King & Volunteer – *£5. 5. 0. One boatman.*

Monday 3 April 1950.
Glen Usk. *Capt. F. Brander.*
08.00. Mardyke Wall to Cumberland Basin under own steam. One boatman.

Tuesday 4 April 1950.
Cold. Showers. Dull.
Glen Usk. *Capt. F. Brander.*
06.40. Departed Basin (Cork Shed).
06.45. Through Upper Lock.
To adjust compass. Land adjuster at Avonmouth.
08.00. Depart Avonmouth for light run to Cardiff.

Wednesday 5 April 1950.
Commence sailings. Cardiff to Weston.

And so the *Glen Usk* began the season; all the other paddle steamers were in service by Whit Sunday, 28 May. The deployment of the ships was different from that of the previous two years; it was decided that one vessel would be sufficient to maintain the south coast service and that ship, for the height of the season from late June to the end of August, would be the *Empress Queen*. The *Britannia* therefore returned to Bristol Channel duties and was based at Cardiff, replacing the *Cardiff Queen* which went to Swansea for the season, while the *Bristol Queen* continued to run the Bristol – down channel sailings.

The Sussex Coast season was opened by the *Glen Gower*. She left Bristol at 10.15 on Wednesday 24 May, under the command of Capt. E.C. Phillips. She anchored off Barry for a few hours owing to steering trouble which developed during compass adjusting but proceeded just after 16.00, passing Hartland Point at 20.00. On Thursday 25 May she passed the Longships Lighthouse at 01.55 and The Lizard at 04.10, with the wind and sea freshening. Later that morning she ran into an easterly gale and rough seas, and at 11.10 when approaching Start Point, altered course for Plymouth; a pilot was boarded who took her to anchor in Plymouth Sound at 12.15. The weather showed no signs of improvement and at 14.50 she was moored at the Plymouth North Pontoon. She sailed again at 03.20 on Friday 26 May, put into Southampton to take on coal, arrived at the Palace Pier, Brighton at 19.35 and eventually reached Newhaven at 20.40 after a journey of 2 days and 10½ hours. She ran her first trips on Whit Sunday 28 May, and continued until Wednesday 21 June, when she left Newhaven to return to the Bristol Channel. She was forced to anchor off Ryde overnight to shelter from stormy south westerly winds but proceeded at 04.25 on the following day and anchored in Cardiff Roads at 07.45 on Friday 23 June. She then shared duties with the *Ravenswood* and *Glen Usk* at Cardiff and Newport. The principal benefit of this was to give a Newport to Ilfracombe sailing at least once a week, usually via Weston, without Newport passengers having to change on to either the Bristol to Ilfracombe or Cardiff to Ilfracombe steamer.

Meanwhile, the *Empress Queen* left Bristol at 11.35 on Thursday 22 June. After compass adjusting off Barry she had to anchor off Ilfracombe at 18.40 owing to an influx of water in her fuel oil. The problem was rectified and she proceeded at 20.10, arriving at Newhaven at 20.30 on the following day in readiness to begin her south coast season on Sunday 25 June.

Off Ilfracombe at 18.45 on Thursday 22 June 1950. The Empress Queen, *on her way from Bristol to Brighton, has just dropped anchor owing to an influx of water in her fuel oil. The* Britannia, *having just returned from Lundy, is leaving for Lynmouth, Barry and Cardiff, and the* Cardiff Queen *is about to make her way to the pier to await her 20.00 departure for Swansea.* (H.G. Owen)

The Empress Queen *arriving at the Palace Pier, Brighton, in 1950. Owing to the appalling weather, her south coast season fared little better than that of the Bristol Channel steamers. In addition to the cancellation of nine complete days' sailings, numerous other trips were abandoned owing to the lack of passengers.* (Chris Collard Collection)

The summer of 1950, from July on, was predominantly one of appalling weather, which naturally had an adverse effect on passenger figures. Another factor detrimental not only to the White Funnel Fleet but to all coastal passenger steamer operators, was the de-rationing of petrol, after ten years on Friday 26 May 1950. This immediately led to a considerable increase in road traffic and the newspapers reported a very busy Whitsun of traffic jams and long queues at garages. Before the war the motor car was the rich man's prerogative but it was an item becoming increasingly more financially accessible to a larger section of the community. This trend, which accelerated as the decade progressed, was one of the major factors in bringing about the decline of the pleasure steamers. The following article, with the headline: 'Big Drop in Pleasure Steamer Bookings', appeared in the *Western Mail* on Thursday 13 July 1950:

> *Although June proved to be a month exceptionally free from rain Monmouthshire folk did not make good use of the pleasure steamer trips from Newport. It was reported to the Newport Harbour Commissioners yesterday that 4,871 passengers used the paddle steamers compared with 8,845 last June.*

All of the steamers experienced a share of the rough weather during that wet and windy season but the worst was that encountered by the *Cardiff Queen* on the exposed Swansea to Ilfracombe route. In July, for example, two days sailings were cancelled completely because of appalling weather conditions and on two other occasions very heavy seas forced her to turn back shortly after leaving Swansea. On the evening of Wednesday 6 September 1950 her return sailing from Ilfracombe to Swansea was cancelled and her passengers were accommodated in hotels for the night. The following morning's crossing was also cancelled but she eventually returned in the evening. Her worst experience however was encountered just before her season was due to end.

On Saturday 16 September 1950 she arrived at Ilfracombe at 16.00 and after disembarking her passengers, anchored in the Range. A southerly gale then developed rapidly, her anchor began to drag and at about 18.30 she berthed at the Stone Bench. The 20.00 return trip to Swansea was cancelled and most of the intending passengers were accommodated in hotels; twelve however, chose to remain on board. For the early part of the night she was high and dry but by the early hours of the following morning she was afloat and ranging violently at the pier. Just after 02.00 on Sunday 17 September the gale increased to hurricane force and the heavy seas sweeping into the harbour caused her to bump on the seabed. The starboard bow struck a concrete landing on the pier and all of her mooring ropes, except that at the stern, parted. By 02.50 steam had been raised, the stern rope was hacked through and she backed out of the harbour. Two attempts were made to anchor but it would not hold and Capt. Murphy decided to steam up channel for shelter. The weather conditions precluded her entering Barry and all the berths at the Pier Head, Cardiff, were full so at 07.30 she anchored off Penarth. Later that morning she made her way to Bristol and the decision was made to end her season a few days early. Those passengers stranded at Ilfracombe made their long way home by train. As for the dozen who had remained on board, a newspaper reported:

> *The part played by the officers and crew in getting the* Cardiff Queen *safely to Bristol on that furious morning has not passed unrecognised. The presentation of a silver cigarette case has been made to her master with the inscription: 'To Captain Albert Murphy of the* Cardiff Queen, *in appreciation of your superb skill in bringing your ship and passengers through the severe gale on Sunday 17 September 1950, without loss or damage. A fine job of work, quietly but magnificently done.'*

The *Bristol Queen*, with Capt. Jack George in command, had also experienced problems. Her sailing from Bristol to Ilfracombe and Lundy, on Wednesday 30 August, came to an abrupt halt when she fell heavily against Weston Pier and cracked her spring beam, bent four paddle floats and forced the star centre out of alignment. After disembarking all of her passengers she left the pier at 10.30 and limped back to Walton Bay where she anchored to await the tide in the River Avon. At 19.00 she hove up and proceeded, arriving at the Underfall Yard at 23.43. She was repaired on the following day and was back in service on Friday 1 September. On the following Saturday evening, returning from Ilfracombe to Bristol, she sailed from Barry at just after 22.00 and made four attempts to land at Weston Pier but was prevented from doing so by the high winds. She had to proceed to Bristol, where she arrived at 01.33 on the following day, her Weston passengers returning home by coaches.

Shortly before the season ended the *Glen Usk* met with difficulties at Weston Pier which were recounted in the log book by her Chief Officer, David Miles. The entry epitomises the trials and frustrations experienced by the officers and crew, weary after their long season and exasperated by the unrelenting, deplorable weather.

Ilfracombe, Saturday 19 August; one of the rare fine days of 1950.

The Bristol Queen *arriving at the pier, after lying at anchor offshore. As Saturdays were the holiday makers' arrival and departure days, cruises out of Ilfracombe were not very well patronised and were the exception rather than the rule.* (H.G. Owen)

The Bristol Queen *is now moored at the Stone Bench, waiting to take her 17.45 return trip to Lynmouth, Barry, Weston, Clevedon and Bristol. Work on the reconstruction of the pier is well under way.* (H.G. Owen)

The Britannia, *like the* Bristol Queen, *has been at anchor offshore and now approaches the pier to take her 18.00 return trip to Lynmouth, Barry, Penarth and Cardiff.* (H.G. Owen)

In the post-war years it was usual for the Swansea steamer to make a morning and afternoon crossing to Ilfracombe on Thursdays, (Swansea's early closing day), and Saturdays. Here the Cardiff Queen *is arriving on her afternoon trip. She will lie at the pier until her 20.00 return journey to Swansea.* (H.G. Owen)

In contrast to the previous photographs, a day much more typical of the summer of 1950. The Glen Gower *has just spent a few uncomfortable hours rolling at anchor off shore, and is seen coming in to the pier to take the 17.30 return trip to Lynmouth, Barry, Weston and Newport. On that day, Thursday 17 August, the* Cardiff Queen's *sailings from Swansea were cancelled.* (H.G. Owen)

Monday 2 October 1950.

The day opened with strong westerly winds, squalls of gale force and heavy rain. South cones were hoisted but vessel did her scheduled run. Wind velocity increased throughout the day to whole gale with vessel rolling, pitching and heaving in heavy, confused seas. Vessel returned to Cardiff Roads at 13.00 for a safe anchorage over the low water period. Vessel held her anchorage and proceeded to Weston at 16.30 to resume her scheduled sailings. At approx. 17.00 whole gale force winds with hurricane force squalls were prevailing and while berthing alongside Weston Pier at 17.30 the six inch rope parted causing the master to back away from the pier in order to re-take it. While backing away vessel shipped heavy seas on the after quarter and waist on the starboard side causing damage to the two wing doors and washing twelve fathoms of rope into the starboard paddle wheel. The second attempt at Weston Pier was successful but while alongside vessel was rolling and ranging about, thereby parting the five inch bow rope; a new one was run out. During the time alongside, the rope which had fouled the starboard wheel Jenny Nettle was cleared and at 18.30, half an hour after the scheduled sailing time, vessel proceeded to Cardiff, arriving there at 19.32. It was then decided by Mr Jack Guy, the Cardiff Agent, that in view of the prevailing weather conditions the vessel's one remaining advertised trip should be cancelled. I consider that the mate and bosun did an excellent job of work in clearing the fouled Jenny Nettle in extremely hazardous circumstances.

Findlay Brander
Master

David Miles
Mate

The grim season drew to its close with the *Glen Usk* making the last ferry crossings on Monday 9 October 1950. The directors report to the shareholders made depressing reading, a part of which stated:

> *From every point of view 1950 was the worst season experienced by the company since its incorporation. The weather during the months of July, August and September was deplorable and its effect on traffic disastrous.*

Passenger figures had fallen by 270,000 to 389,000. The profit of £64,000 in 1949 had become a loss of £35,000, takings dropping by over £90,000. Expenses had increased by £10,000, a great deal of which had been brought about by cancelled trips, steamers running for shelter and the extra costs incurred in getting people home by alternative transport as well as hotel bills for those occasions when passengers were stranded overnight.

The report also referred to the decision to withdraw sailings from Brighton in the following year. The *Empress Queen* had not been a success on the south coast, partly because berthing at the piers was such a slow process which led to erratic timekeeping, but mainly because she seemed to be impossible to fill with sufficient passengers. The bad weather added to her problems causing the cancellation of nine days sailings. Cross-channel trips seemed to be as far away as ever and she was described by the chairman as 'a source of anxiety because, from an economic point of view, it is very difficult to run her as a coastwise steamer'. Once again alternative employment had to be found for her in the hope of making her pay.

The Directors considered the possibility of purchasing a small vessel to maintain the Sussex Coast sailings and an amount of £50,000 was authorised for this purpose but it was soon realised that this was an insufficient sum for such a purpose and the idea was abandoned.

The company looked forward to the following year and hoped for a better season but it was not to be.

1951 was the year of the Festival of Britain. An area of the South Bank of the Thames was cleared of its war time ruins to make way for the Festival Hall, the Exhibition Centre, and other examples of contemporary architecture. Opened on Friday 4 May 1951 by King George VI, it symbolised hope for the future and attempted to dispel the gloom which then pervaded the country, still in the grip of austerity and rationing. Economic uncertainty caused much concern in all walks of life, not least in the coastal passenger trade and in the Bristol Channel, hopes of a profitable season were being dashed once again by bad weather.

The Whitsun weekend was, however, very good; in fact, on Whit-Monday the *Glen Usk*, with Capt. Brander again in command, left Weston at 19.30 three quarters of an hour before her scheduled sailing time, with a full complement of 1,162 passengers. She had to make an additional ferry crossing, leaving Cardiff at 23.12, to bring home the large number of people returning from Weston.

A highlight of an otherwise indifferent season was the re-opening of Minehead as a port of call. The pier had been completely demolished, on Military orders, during the war. There were plans to rebuild it with the Government bearing the main burden of the cost, stated to

Next Page: Aboard the Ravenswood *at Clevedon Pier on a Sunday afternoon in 1951.* (W.T. Collard)

The Glen Gower *at the Mardyke Wharf, Bristol, shortly before her 1951 season.* (H.G. Owen)

The Britannia *arriving at Weston in 1951. In the background the* Glen Usk *can be seen leaving for Cardiff.* (W.T. Collard)

The Glen Gower *has just passed beneath the Transporter Bridge, on the River Usk, on an afternoon cruise to Bristol. 1951.* (Chris Collard Collection)

have been in excess of £70,000, but at the beginning of the decade steel shortages were still acute and the Government eventually withdrew its support. The Minehead Urban District Council was not in a position to finance such an undertaking but, as an alternative, arranged for the shingle patch in the old harbour to be dredged to give sufficient depth for the steamers to berth at the stone jetty. The *Glen Usk* was the first to call, on Saturday 2 June 1951. She left Cardiff at 14.30, called at Penarth and arrived at Minehead at 16.40. Fortunately the weather was fine and a large number of residents and local dignitaries, as well as holiday-makers lined the picturesque harbour and jetty to greet her. After a welcoming ceremony she left for a cruise towards Watchet returning to Minehead at 17.45 before departing, at 18.20, for Weston, Penarth and Cardiff.

Calls at Minehead often took the form of afternoon trips from Cardiff, Penarth and Barry, with an extending cruise, usually to Porlock Bay but sometimes to off Watchet. Many of these trips were performed by the *Ravenswood*, her cruises to Porlock Bay being the limit of her post-war sailings down the English coast.

The *Ravenswood* was in the news on Friday 22 June 1951. She left Weston at 20.10 for Newport, with Capt. W.F. Watson in command, and at 20.57, in the vicinity of the West Usk Buoy near the mouth of the River Usk, had to put about and stem the flood tide. One of her firemen was drunk and totally incapable, resulting in the steam pressure falling to about a half of its correct level. Her speed therefore dropped and she would have had little steerage way for the passage up the Usk, a situation which could have led to disastrous consequences. She circled at the mouth of the river until 21.12, when sufficient steam had been raised for her to proceed. She arrived at Newport at 21.45 and the log book records that at 22.55 the offending fireman was arrested!

The Cardiff Queen *leaving Swansea in 1951.* (Chris Collard Collection)

Aboard the Bristol Queen, *bound for Ilfracombe, passing the* Glen Usk *making her way up 'the drain' to the Pier Head, Cardiff in 1951.* (Seaton Phillips)

The resumption of sailings to Minehead was a highlight of an otherwise indifferent season. The Glen Usk *is seen at the opening ceremony on Saturday 2 June 1951.* (Chris Collard Collection)

She was in the news again on Wednesday 25 July 1951 when she left Barry at 19.34, steamed stern first between the breakwaters and collided with the Newport Pilot Cutter *Belle Usk* coming into the harbour. She stopped for her rudder to be examined but proceeded to Weston at 19.49 apparently undamaged.

Much discussion had taken place concerning the employment of the *Empress Queen* for the 1951 season. Eventually arrangements were made for her to sail from Torquay; she was to run a service to the Channel Islands three times per week, with coastal cruises on the intervening days, Saturdays being off service days. On Thursday 14 June 1951 she embarked 112 passengers in Avonmouth Dock for the round trip. Under the command of Capt. J.A. Kidd, she left her berth at 13.37, but while manoeuvring she struck the quay wall twice with her stern, damaging her counter and stern frame, mostly above the waterline. She returned to the berth where her passengers disembarked and returned to Bristol by bus. At 13.00 on the following day the *Empress Queen* left Avonmouth for Bristol and entered Hill's Dry Dock for repairs. These were completed by Saturday 23 June when she left the Cumberland Basin for South Devon. Her first crossing to the Channel Islands took place on Monday 25 June 1951, when she left Torquay at 09.20 in fine weather with 198 passengers aboard, arriving at Guernsey at 13.40.

Her season ended with a final day trip to Guernsey on Wednesday 12 September 1951, with 621 passengers. She had made a total of thirty-two such trips; the crossing took about 4½ hours and allowed about three hours ashore. The fare was 32/6 and for an additional 6/- passengers could avail themselves of a motor coach tour of the island. An average of 505 passengers were carried per trip, her two best days being Wednesday 1 and Wednesday 8 August when she carried exactly 1,000 passengers per trip. She also ran three-day-return trips to Alderney but these proved to be much less popular, her complement of passengers averaging a mere 137.

The damage to the stern of the Empress Queen *sustained when leaving her berth in Avonmouth Dock for Torquay on Thursday 14 June 1951.* (H.G. Owen Collection)

The Empress Queen *in Torquay harbour on one of her many out of service days in 1951. She had been fitted with radar for the season at a cost of £2,250. The scanner can be seen on top of the wheel-house.* (Edwin Keen)

The Ravenswood *at the Landing Stage, Newport, in the early 1950s.* (John Ruddle).

The coastal trips, on the intervening days, were disastrous! Her most successful cruise took place on Sunday 1 July when, although she carried only fifty passengers from Torquay to Weymouth, she then took 420 from Weymouth to Bournemouth. On the four following coastal trips, all of them non-landing cruises, she carried an average of only 108 passengers. After the last of these, on Sunday 15 July, all further coastal trips were abandoned as being totally uneconomical.

She left Torquay on Sunday 16 September and arrived at Bristol on the following day. Her log book for the season no longer exists but the memorandum book records that, during her period in South Devon from Monday 23 June to Sunday 16 September, no less than forty-two sailing days were lost because of a combination of the aborted coastal cruises, repairs, off service days and bad weather. The equivalent of six weeks lost in a twelve week season was, of course, financially untenable and proved to be the last straw. With cross channel trips to France still out of the question there was no alternative other than to lay the ship up. She was moored at Narrow Quay, City Centre, Bristol where, only four years earlier, she had been proudly displayed to the citizens of her home port for the first time.

The season continued relatively uneventfully until the *Glen Usk* developed a leak in the engine room caused by a slack rivet in the bottom of her hull which necessitated the cancellation of her sailings for repairs on Sunday 9 September. Further cancellations were caused by severe gales in mid-September and the generally indifferent weather led to detrimental passenger figures; the trading loss for the season amounting to £7,410.

1952/1953 – The Tides Turn

The 1952 season began with a potential disaster. The *Glen Usk*, having commenced sailings just before Easter, collided with a cabin cruiser off Penarth on Sunday 27 April 1952. The details are quoted from Capt. Brander's report:

> *At 11.02, when the vessel left Penarth Pier in dense fog, with 167 passengers, in a calm sea, coming around to her course of SE 3/4 E the three look-out men posted forward jointly reported a boat ahead. The master was sounding the whistle at this instant and immediately put the vessel full speed astern to avoid collision. Visibility at the time was nil and the vessel unavoidably struck the boat amidships with her stem. Speed of vessel at the time was slow to half ahead.*
>
> *No audible sound of bell or horn was heard from the boat until it appeared under the bow. The boat drifted away in the fog, in a sinking condition. Two men who manned her came up over the vessel's bow, the remaining two men and a boy took to the water.*
>
> *The vessel's look-outs and remainder of the crew ran aft to launch the emergency boat, on the way aft five lifebuoys were cast adrift and were used by the men in the water. At 11.08 the emergency boat was in the water and rowed off a short distance from the vessel's stern to pick up the men and boy; at 11.12 the boat was alongside the sponson and they were put in the care of the Chief Steward. Only the boy appeared to be suffering from shock. Ordinary Seaman Peter King gallantly dived overboard and assisted the boy into the lifeboat. The men and boy were taken to Weston and landed at Penarth Pier on the return trip. An interview of the owner of the boat revealed that she was a 36ft. converted motor boat, ex. Naval, named* Katrina.

The Ravenswood *and* Britannia *in the Merchant's Dock, Bristol, shortly before the beginning of the 1952 season.* (W.T. Collard)

The boy, twelve- year-old Michael Manley, was unable to swim and undoubtedly would have drowned had it not been for the seaman's prompt action. Some time later the crew of the *Glen Usk* and the occupants of the *Katrina* were entertained to tea by the Lord Mayor and Lady Mayoress at the City Hall, Cardiff. In recognition of his gallant action Peter King was presented with a wristwatch by Michael Manley, and also a cheque and an inscribed silver salver by the company's managing director, Mr W G. Banks

On the day following the *Glen Usk's* collision, Monday 28 April, the *Bristol Queen* was towed from Bristol to Avonmouth for dry-docking. While being manoeuvred she hit the quay wall and sustained considerable damage to her stem. She was in dry dock until Friday 9 May for the necessary repairs to be effected in addition to the normal pre-season preparations.

A further blow fell at the beginning of May 1952 when the death was announced of Capt. Daniel Taylor, of Stoke Bishop, Bristol. He had been associated with the company for over fifty years. Capt. Taylor was eighty-eight and had retired about twenty years earlier, having first arrived in Bristol, from Scotland, in 1891. Over the years his knowledge and experience of the Bristol Channel became legendary and he was, without doubt, one of the Company's most respected masters.

On a brighter note, Ilfracombe's newly renovated pier was opened on the afternoon of Saturday 31 May 1952 by Earl Fortescue, Lord Lieutenant of Devon. This was the triumphant culmination of a three-year struggle against economic uncertainties, shortages of materials and the forces of nature, such as long periods of rough weather. Before cutting the white

Lifeboat drill aboard the Glen Gower *in the Cumberland Basin, Wednesday 28 May 1952. Before beginning their seasons, the crew of each of the steamers were exercised in fire drill and in launching and manning the lifeboats, under the scrutiny of a Board of Trade examiner. They were not signed on articles unless a certificate of competency had been obtained.* (Cyril Hawkins Garrington)

ribbon and declaring the pier open, Earl Fortescue traced the history of the Ilfracombe Harbour undertaking. He commended all those responsible for the building of the new structure and paid particular tribute to the consulting engineers, Messrs Deane and Mason, the contractors, Messrs A.E. Farr Ltd. and to the workmen, many of them local, who had quickly adapted themselves to the exacting demands of the specialised operations.

The *Glen Usk* arrived at the pier at 16.20, shortly after the opening ceremony had ended. Her master, Capt. Brander, went ashore and was greeted by Earl Fortescue and the Chairman of the Ilfracombe Council. The official party, accompanied by about 350 children, were then taken on a cruise towards Lynmouth at the invitation of the company.

The disposal of the ships in 1952 was somewhat different. The *Ravenswood*, (Capt. W.F. Watson), the *Glen Gower*, (Capt. A.V. Murphy), and *Bristol Queen*, (Capt. J. George), were out by Whit-Sunday 1 June and joined the *Glen Usk* up channel. On Tuesday 24 June the *Glen Gower* was transferred to Swansea, leaving only three ships up channel until the *Britannia*, (Capt. J.A. Harris), appeared, very late because of extensive maintenance, on Sunday 6 July.

The Sussex Coast sailings were re-instated by the *Cardiff Queen*, for the first time in her career, for a fairly short season. She made only one sailing in the Bristol Channel, from Bristol to Cardiff and Ilfracombe, on Saturday 21 June, the day before she left Bristol for Brighton under the command of Capt. E.C. Phillips. Her timings for the round trip were as follows:

Sunday 22 June 1952.
06.30 Left Cumberland Basin.
07.32 Left Pontoon.
11.49 Left Ilfracombe.

The Cardiff Queen *returning to Bristol from Ilfracombe on Saturday 21 June 1952; her only Bristol Channel sailing that season. She is swinging at Tongue Head on an ebb tide before entering the Cumberland Basin for the night. On the following morning she left for the south coast.* (Edwin Keen)

13.16 Passed Hartland Point.
15.37 Passed Trevose Head.
20.18 Passed The Lizard.
23.36 Plymouth Pilot boarded.

Monday 23 June 1952.
00.10 Arrived at Plymouth for re-fuelling.
03.00 Left Plymouth.
08.19 Passed Portland.
10.10 Passed The Needles.
14.03 Arrived Palace Pier, Brighton.
13.07 Arrived at Newhaven.

A highlight of the South Coast season was the arrival, at Southampton, of the new American liner *United States*. On Thursday 3 July 1952 she left New York at noon, passing the Ambrose Light Vessel at 14.36. At 06.16 on Monday 7 July she passed the Bishop Rock Lighthouse, Isles of Scilly, after a record crossing, thus taking the Blue Riband of the Atlantic. Her average speed of 35.59 knots was 3.9 knots faster than that of the *Queen Mary* on the previous record breaking journey of 1938. The *United States*, after an overnight stay at Le Havre, arrived at

Aboard the Ravenswood *passing beneath the Clifton Suspension Bridge in 1952. Her master, Captain George Gunn, keeps a watchful eye from the starboard bridge wing.* (Seaton Phillips)

The Cardiff Queen *at Newhaven in 1952.* (Chris Collard Collection)

Southampton on the afternoon of Tuesday 8 July to a tumultuous welcome at which the *Cardiff Queen* was present, on a cruise from Hastings, Eastbourne, Brighton and Worthing. The liner proved to be a major attraction on her first and subsequent visits and helped to boost the passenger figures on the already popular cruises to Southampton Water.

In the Bristol Channel, the *Bristol Queen* was out of service from Thursday 24 July to Monday 28 July with engine trouble. The *Glen Gower* was withdrawn from the Swansea station to replace her up channel and she, in turn, was replaced at Swansea by the *Britannia*.

The *Glen Gower* experienced a difficult weekend in early August. It was usual for the Swansea steamer to have an off service day on a Friday but owing to heavy advanced bookings she made an extra crossing to Ilfracombe, in a fresh to moderate SW wind, on Friday 8 August. Overnight the wind increased to gale force and continued into the following morning when her first crossing to Ilfracombe was cancelled because her firemen went on strike as a protest against losing their day off. She sailed on the afternoon trip at 13.35 and headed out past Mumbles Head into a very heavy sea. Capt. Murphy reduced speed but when three miles WSW of the Scarweather Light Vessel, one hour and ten minutes out of Swansea, he considered it prudent to turn back. By that time the tide was too low for her to return up the River Tawe so she had to anchor in Swansea Bay. While heaving up at 18.00 she picked up a 9in cable in the flukes of the anchor which had to be sawn through; she eventually arrived in Swansea at 18.35.

Conditions were very bad up channel that evening when the *Glen Usk* was delayed, firstly by the *Bristol Queen's* abortive attempts to berth at Weston Pier and then by having to make three attempts at it herself! During the night the company's motor launch, *Cambria* was swept from her moorings at Lundy and destroyed by the heavy seas.

On the following morning, with the wind still blowing hard from the west and a very heavy swell running, the *Glen Gower* left Swansea at 09.00, cancelled the advertised call at Porthcawl, slowed down on the passage across and arrived at Ilfracombe at 11.50, where a large crowd on the pier were awaiting the arrival of the steamers. The *Bristol Queen* arrived from Bristol and

The Glen Usk *leaving Weston, having just disembarked 1,115 passengers from Cardiff and Penarth. The* Bristol Queen *approaches, with 687 passengers from Clevedon and Bristol, on her way to Barry, Lynmouth and Ilfracombe, Tuesday 22 July 1952.* (Norman Bird)

In 1952 the Glen Gower *was the Swansea steamer. However, owing to the fact that the* Bristol Queen *was out of service for boiler repairs from 24 to 28 July, and that heavy advanced bookings had been made for that weekend, the* Glen Gower's *large passenger carrying capacity was required at Cardiff. She therefore changed places with the* Britannia *for four days. The latter is seen here heading down the River Tawe, bound for Porthcawl and Ilfracombe on the morning of Sunday 27 July 1952.* (H.G. Owen)

Low tide at Ilfracombe in 1952. The Britannia *lies on the sand at the Stone Bench.* (H.G. Owen)

The Glen Gower *arriving at Penarth Pier, during the early 1950s. Captain Phillips is at the telegraphs and at the wheel is Chief Officer J.W. (Jack) Harris, who later became her master.* (Chris Collard Collection)

set off for Lundy but put back when just west of Bull Point because of the very rough seas.

The following weekend brought further bad weather but with much more serious consequences. On Friday 15 August 1952 rain began to fall heavily over south west England. On Exmoor it was particularly heavy and after an incredible nine inches had fallen, five inches in five hours at one period, the streams turned into torrents. The West Lyn River diverted from its course in Lynmouth and a wall of water carrying boulders, trees and other debris swept through the main street of the village in an unremitting mass, destroying everything in its path. Three million pounds worth of damage was caused by the flood which carried away seventeen bridges; destroyed thirty three houses and damaged others; took ninety-five cars, some of which were swept into the sea; and killed over thirty people. One Civic leader remarked, 'In the darkness of a single night a part of Lynmouth has vanished forever'. It was rated as the greatest natural disaster in Great Britain at the time. The steamers ceased calling at Lynmouth from the following day. The company donated one hundred guineas to the local council and collections were made on board the ships throughout the remainder of the season which were donated to the flood disaster fund.

The company's launch *Westward Ho* was lost on this occasion and in further wild weather, which occurred early in September, a third launch, *Devonia*, was lost off Lundy. On the same day, Tuesday 9 September, the *Bristol Queen* sailed from Bristol, Clevedon and Weston for Ilfracombe but when she reached there the heavy seas and gale force winds prevented her from berthing at the pier and she returned up channel, having given her passengers only a brief glimpse of their intended destination.

The *Cardiff Queen* finished her south coast season on Tuesday 16 September 1952. She left Newhaven at 06.36 on Thursday 18 September and arrived at Plymouth for refuelling at 19.25. She then left Plymouth at 06.00 on the following day, and after a smooth passage made a slight detour and anchored off Lundy at 17.10 to pick up personnel and supplies for the mainland. Owing to the loss of the Lundy launches, one of the *Cardiff Queen's* lifeboats had to be used, but difficulties in launching it, the temporary breakdown of its motor, and the trials of getting a rather 'high' deer carcass aboard caused several hours delay. This meant that she would miss the tide at Cardiff, her scheduled destination. Therefore, after landing the Lundy personnel and cargo at Ilfracombe, she left at 00.20 on Saturday 20 September, disembarked her passengers at Barry at 06.00 and then sailed direct to Bristol!

The 1952 season ended on Monday 6 October and was later reviewed at the company's Annual General Meeting. The Chairman, Mr A.R. Boucher reported an operating profit of £4,861, compared with the loss of about £7,500 for 1951 but said that the bad weather during 1952 had adversely affected the trading position. In answer to calls for reduced fares and catering charges Mr Boucher said that the board constantly had the matter under review and that, in the following season, fares were being reduced on the south coast as an experiment. Hit by a bad August and September after an extremely good start, the company had suffered a further setback with the *Bristol Queen* being off service with engine trouble for a week and the loss of the launches at Lynmouth and Lundy. During the meeting it was announced that the former Managing Director, Mr W.J. Banks, would be resigning from the Board. The Chairman paid tribute to his fifty-six years of service with the company and added that he would still serve in a technical capacity.

Whereas 1950 to 1952 were years of anxiety, unalleviated it seemed, by much hope of improvement in the immediate future, 1953 suddenly and unexpectedly blossomed as a year of encouraging prospects, mainly owing to greater economic stability. This, combined with major events such as the conquest of Mount Everest and the Coronation of Queen Elizabeth II, gave the population a lift out of its post war gloom.

The year, however, started badly. In February the British Railways Motor Vessel *Princess Victoria* sank while on passage from Stranraer to Larne in a severe storm. There was speculation that the *Empress Queen* might have been purchased by BR to replace her, she having been engaged so succesfully on that route during the war, but no such sale took place.

The *Empress Queen* had been advertised for sale, a selling price of £120,000 to £125,000 having been decided upon as acceptable by the board. She had been inspected in February 1953 by representatives of the Hamburg-Amerika Line but no offer was forthcoming and she remained laid up in the City Centre, Bristol.

Coronation Day was Tuesday 2 June 1953 and in the months that followed an extensive round of tours and visits was planned for the Queen and members of the Royal Family, one of which was the Naval Review held at Spithead on Monday 15 June 1953. The Queen and Duke of Edinburgh, in the frigate HMS *Surprise,* temporarily in use as the Royal Yacht, sailed through the fleet of warships and merchant vessels, including the last British battleship, *Vanguard,* nine aircraft carriers, ten cruisers and other ships from sixteen navies. Never again would so large a fleet be assembled in home waters.

As always, such events were major sources of revenue for the steamers. That year the *Cardiff Queen* made no Bristol Channel sailings but went to the Sussex Coast for the second and last time. She opened the season on Saturday 23 May and made the first post war calls at Ventnor on Whit-Monday 25 May, and Folkestone on Wednesday 24 June.

At the Coronation Naval Review the White Funnel Fleet was represented by three steamers, the *Cardiff Queen* being joined by the *Glen Gower* and *Bristol Queen.* The three ships ran cruises to see the fleet assembling prior to their being chartered, like many other British pleasure and cross channel steamers, to act as 'Grandstands' for the actual Review. Their activities are summarised in diary form.

Glen Gower
Wednesday 10 June to Sunday 14 June 1953.
Cruises in Spithead from Brighton and Eastbourne.
Monday 15 June 1953.
On charter to Dean & Dawson Ltd, 450 passengers at a cost of £3,800.
From Newhaven. Cruise in Spithead.
Anchored for the Review.
Tuesday 16 June 1933.
Returned to Newhaven in the early hours of the morning.
Wednesday 17 June 1933.
Left Newhaven at 09.00 to return to the Bristol Channel.

Cardiff Queen
Thursday 11 June.
Cruise in Spithead from Brighton and Worthing
Friday 12 June.
Cruise in Spithead from Hastings and Eastbourne
Saturday 13 June.
Cruise in Spithead from Brighton. Then light from Brighton, at 1900, to Southampton, arriving at 23.30
Sunday 14 June
Off service at Southampton
Monday 15 June 1953.
On charter to Frarres Tours Ltd.
450 passengers at a cost of £3,750.
10.07 Dep. Southampton on cruise through lines of ships.
12.00 Anchored for the Review.
17.55 Hove up anchor and cruised through lines of ships.
20.55 Anchored for fireworks.
23.40 Hove up and proceeded.
Tuesday 16 June 1953.
00.50 Arrived at Southampton.
05.00 Dep. Southampton.
09.45 Arr. Newhaven.

Bristol Queen
Saturday 13 June 1953.
10.17 Dep. Southampton.
12.39 Arr. Bournemouth.
13.35 Dep. Bournemouth on cruise through lines of ships. (Combined with a rail connection from Bristol).
Sunday 14 June 1953. Off service in Southampton.
Monday 15 June 1953. On charter to Thomas Cook & Son Ltd with a private party from

English Electric Ltd at a cost of £3,900.
09.32 Dep. Southampton on cruise through lines of ships.
12.24 Anchored for the Review.
18.00 Hove up anchor and cruised through lines of ships.
20.52 Anchored for fireworks.
23.38 Hove up and proceeded.
Tuesday 16 June 1953.
01.10 Arr. at Southampton.
Wednesday 17 June 1953.
Left Southampton at 10.30 to return to the Bristol Channel.

After completing her south coast season the *Cardiff Queen* had a most eventful voyage home. On Saturday 19 September 1953 she left Newhaven at 06.17 and Palace Pier, Brighton at 08.01 in a flat calm sea and hot, sultry air on the first part of her journey, to Plymouth. A few hours later the wind began to freshen and by early evening it had increased to gale force with heavy squalls. One of her passengers, Norman Bird, stated:

> *I have often admired the toughness of P&A Campbell's officers facing all weathers on the open bridges of their ships, but never as much as on this occasion. The seas broke across* Cardiff Queen*'s bridge and swept her promenade deck. After dark we could sometimes see the distant lights of the Devon shore as we rode on to the crest of a wave, then they were completely lost as we descended into a trough. The* Cardiff Queen *shook and rattled her way through it all and was only two hours late arriving at Plymouth.*

On the following day she left Plymouth at 09.40, four hours later than intended, in the hope

The Bristol Queen *at Bournemouth Pier, en route from Plymouth to Southampton, Thursday 11 June 1953.* (Edwin Keen)

The Cardiff Queen *at her allotted anchorage in Spithead on Naval Review Day, Monday 15 June 1953.* (Chris Collard Collection)

that the weather would moderate sufficiently for her to negotiate the turbulent waters off Lands End. It was gloriously sunny that morning but the sea conditions were still very bad and in view of the fact that further imminent gales from the south-west were forecast just before she reached The Lizard, Capt. Phillips decided to put into Falmouth for shelter; her only visit to that port. Most of her passengers disembarked and returned home by train and it was not until Wednesday 23 September that the weather moderated sufficiently for the *Cardiff Queen* to resume her voyage to Bristol. She left Falmouth at 16.30 and entered the Cumberland Basin at 10.40 on Thursday 24 September after a total journey time from Newhaven to Bristol, of five days, four hours and twenty-three minutes.

The Bristol Channel sailings had progressed with little incident, apart from the *Ravenswood* having to be dry-docked for a few days in July for repairs to a minor leak in her hull.

The *Britannia* had been the Swansea steamer for the whole of the 1953 season, the only time in her career. On Saturday 19 September her morning trip to Ilfracombe was cancelled because of paddle trouble. An interesting entry in the memorandum book reads:

> *Driving arm fractured. This is believed to be the first time one of* Brit's *original wheel spares will be required in fifty-seven years.*

Another season of indifferent weather meant that business had not been good and the trading loss for the year amounted to £12,627.

The general trend towards private motoring continued and in the autumn of 1953 a price war between motor manufacturers brought even greater accessibility of the motor car to an increasing number of families. It was at that time that Ford introduced the 'Popular', the cheapest car of the time, at a cost, including purchase tax, of £390!

The Cardiff Queen *stormbound at the Trinity Pier, Plymouth, on Sunday 20 September 1953.* (John Brown collection)

The Cardiff Queen *stormbound at Falmouth on Monday 21 September 1953.* (Chris Collard Collection)

The Empress Queen *laid up at Narrow Quay, City Centre, Bristol, in September 1953. When she arrived at Bristol from Torquay on the morning of Monday 17 September 1951, the* Empress Queen *was moored at the Mardyke Wharf, but once the decision had been made to lay her up, she was moved to Narrow Quay. She was taken in tow by the tugs* Sea Gem *and* John King *on Wednesday 24 October 1951. At this berth she was out of the way of most other shipping movements, but being close to the City Centre, became something of a landmark to the citizens of Bristol for over three years.* (H.G. Owen Collection)

The Britannia *in the Merchant's Dock, Bristol, at the end of the 1953 season.* (Donald Anderson)

1954/1956 – New Channels

1954 marked a turning point in the history of P&A Campbell Ltd. Urgent measures needed to be taken to reverse the declining fortunes of the preceding seasons and a management committee was constituted to address the problems and formulate their solutions. The committee comprised:

Mr S.C. Smith-Cox, Committee Chairman.
Mr W.G. Banks, Company Managing Director.
Mr R. Campbell, Company Director.
Mr J.W. Jenkins, Company Secretary and Director.
Mr J.H. Guy, Traffic Manager.
Mr J. MacGregor, Works Manager.
Capt. J.A. Harris, Marine Superintendent.
Mr J.B. McDougall, South Coast Manager.

The committee's chairman, Sydney Clifton Smith-Cox, was a forty-four-year-old Chartered Accountant. He had been a lifelong enthusiast of the Bristol Channel steamers and was invited to join the Board of Directors in March 1952. In January 1954 he was appointed Joint Managing Director with Mr W.G. Banks and became sole Managing Director from 1 November 1954, when Mr Banks relinquished his post.

Among the management committee's first recommendations were the reopening of further ports of call in the Bristol Channel and on the south coast. More strenuous efforts were to be made to attract the public to the steamers. Publicity was revised, improved and increased. More attractive posters appeared and the timetables were enlarged to give more comprehensive details of the sailings and to include a map and itineraries of the routes. Many fares were reduced and weekly tickets were to be made available at a cost of 35/- for unlimited travel except on Saturdays. Season tickets were introduced for shareholders at a cost of 7 guineas, single or 12 guineas for a double, allowing the holder to take a guest. A wide variety of combined steamer/bus and steamer/rail trips were more fully advertised and greater efforts were made to increase party bookings with details of the facilities available for factory or office outings being circulated to many employers on both sides of the channel.

1954 was designated as the company's 'Centenary Year', the timetables carrying the heading: 'The first steamer built for the Campbells, named *Express*, sailed on the Clyde in 1854. The Bristol Channel service commenced 1887. Limited Company 1893.' During the course of the season the World Ship Society staged an exhibition of steamer photographs, relics and memorabilia in the Bristol City Museum and a demonstration of working models of the *Devonia* and *Glen Usk* took place on St. George's Park Lake, Bristol, on Saturday 31 July. Both events added considerably to the publicity drive.

For the forthcoming season the management committee recommended that the company should charter the General Steam Navigation Co.'s motor vessel *Rochester Queen*, 315 gross tons, for service on short local trips on the south coast, at a charter fee of £6,000. The Board agreed to the proposal and it was decided that she should commence running on Saturday 22 May under the command of Capt. J.W. Harris, former Chief Officer of the *Glen Gower* and *Cardiff Queen*. Tentative plans were also made for the *Cardiff Queen* to leave Bristol on Thursday 17 June to commence service on the longer south coast sailings. However, the Brighton Marine Palace Pier Co. refused to allow the *Rochester Queen* to sail from the pier. A small, locally owned motor vessel called *Anzio* was already running short cruises from Brighton and they were unwilling to accept a second ship similarly employed. The charter was therefore cancelled.

In the meantime it had been decided to allocate the *Glen Gower* to the south coast and not the *Cardiff Queen* owing to developments in the question of day trips to Boulogne. The *Cardiff Queen* was unable to obtain the Board of Trade No.2 certificate which would allow her to cross the channel. The construction of the *Glen Gower* however, gave her the necessary qualifications to make such journeys as, in fact, she had frequently done in the pre-war years. At the directors meeting on Thursday 29 October 1953 a letter was read which had been received from the General Steam Navigation Co. who, like P&A Campbell Ltd, were pressing for permission to run 'no passport' trips to France, in which it was noted that 'the Ministry of Transport state that there is no chance of the resumption of 'no passport' excursions next season.'

However, at the end of May 1954, Mr Banks reported on his negotiations with various Government departments regarding day excursions to Boulogne, with passports. The trips were to start and end at Newhaven with no intermediate calls, rail connections however were to be arranged from the surrounding area. They would be timed to leave Newhaven at 09.30, arriving at Boulogne at 14.00, with a departure at 18.00 to arrive at Newhaven at 22.45. The steamer fare would be 38/6 and either 40/- or 42/- for the combined rail/steamer ticket depending on the point of departure. Full passports would be essential and no duty free or tax-free concessions would be allowed. The maximum amount of sterling permitted to be taken out of the UK was to be £5 and the Westminster Bank were to operate a currency exchange office on the steamer. The board agreed to these proposals but felt that they should continue to press the Government for permission to dispense with the passport restriction.

Incidentally, Mr J.B. McDougall, the south coast manager, reported to the board that permission had been obtained for the *Glen Gower* to call at Littlehampton during 1954, but no such sailings materialised.

For the first time since 1947 two steamers were in service at Easter; the *Glen Usk*, which began on Thursday 15 April, under the command of Capt. Findlay Brander and the *Glen Gower*, which began on Good Friday 16 April, under the command of Capt. E.C. Phillips. Both steamers visited Ilfracombe during the fine Easter weekend after which the *Glen Gower* returned to lay up in Bristol, leaving the *Glen Usk* to maintain the ferry alone.

Prior to the beginning of the season the two *Glens*, in company with the *Ravenswood* and the *Britannia* had been fitted with full mainmasts in order to carry the navigation lights necessary to comply with the new regulations for the 'Prevention of Collision at Sea'. The two *Queens* had already been so fitted as built.

The *Glen Gower* resumed sailing for a few days at the end of May before leaving the Bristol Channel for the south coast on Wednesday 2 June. On the same day the *Cardiff Queen*, commanded by Capt. George Gunn, entered service and resumed calls at Lynmouth, the village having been rebuilt after the disastrous floods of August 1952.

During the night of Thursday 3 June the *Cardiff Queen* lay at Ilfracombe pier in readiness for an early start next morning on the first trip to Bideford since 1924. She left the pier at 07.02, picked up her pilot off the Bar at the mouth of the River Torridge and arrived at Bideford at 08.25. The local press gave the event full coverage:

With her newly-fitted mainmast, the Ravenswood *leaves Weston early in the 1954 season.* (Viv Davies)

The Ravenswood *arriving at Barry on Saturday 19 June 1954. Barry Pier was the only up-channel landing place which could be used at low tide, and the ferry steamer frequently berthed there over the low water period, thus affording her crew a few hours rest. During the busy part of the season, however, a cruise out of Barry would be included in the steamer's itinerary, either to off Minehead, around the Breaksea lightvessel or, as on this particular day, along the Welsh coast towards Nash Point.* (Edwin Keen)

> *After a lapse of thirty years, the port of Bideford was yesterday morning reopened to Bristol Channel passenger traffic.*
>
> *In full civic regalia, the Deputy Mayor, Mr C.A. Grant, and members of the Corporation welcomed the passenger steamer* Cardiff Queen *as she drew alongside the quay.*
>
> *Hundreds of people lined Bideford Quay and all the way down the Torridge, from windows, shipyards and quays, handkerchiefs fluttered and hands waved in a demonstration of goodwill.*
>
> *Underneath a decorated archway of bunting with galleon motifs on each pinnacle the Deputy Mayor welcomed Mr A.R. Boucher, chairman of P&A Campbell Ltd, Mr S.C. Smith-Cox, joint Managing Director, Capt. J.A. Harris, Marine Superintendent and Capt. G.S. Gunn of the* Cardiff Queen.
>
> *Mr W.H. Short, Chairman of the Harbour Committee stated that he thought it fitting that the firm should be reviving its Bideford service in the hundredth year of its existence.*
>
> *Dwarfing the two coasters berthed ahead of her the* Cardiff Queen *was slowly turned about. This operation, difficult in a tidal river, was hampered by an unfavourable breeze but, at 09.15, the* Cardiff Queen *had a rousing send-off as she steamed down the Torridge bound for Swansea with the civic party on board.*

She called at Ilfracombe and then crossed to Swansea where the members of the Bideford Corporation were entertained to lunch by the Mayor and Corporation of Swansea. The return journey began at 18.04, arriving at Bideford at 21.30, after which the *Cardiff Queen* returned once again to Swansea.

The Cardiff Queen *has boarded her pilot and crossed Bideford Bar, the sand bank at the mouth of the River Torridge. She is seen passing the picturesque, ship-building village of Appledore.* (Chris Collard Collection)

The local residents having turned out in force to greet her, the Cardiff Queen *arrives at Bideford Quay.* (Chris Collard Collection)

With Bideford's famous arched bridge just visible in the background, the Cardiff Queen *swings in the river.* (Chris Collard Collection)

In reply to the rousing send off, Captain Gunn gives a blast on the whistle as the Cardiff Queen *sets off for Ilfracombe and Swansea.* (Chris Collard Collection)

On Whit-Saturday 5 June, the *Ravenswood*, with Capt. Leo Virgo, and the *Bristol Queen* with Capt. Jack George, entered service. The Whitsun weekend was one of strong winds which continued over the next few days. On the south coast, the *Glen Gower* managed to make the first post war trip to Sandown, Isle of Wight, on Whit-Monday 7 June before gales caused the cancellation of her next four days sailings.

The *Britannia,* with Capt. Albert Murphy in command, entered service for what was to be a very short season on Monday 28 June and on Thursday 1 July made the first post war call at Portishead, on her way from Bristol to Ilfracombe. On the following evening, while approaching the pontoon at Barry, she had to take evasive action to avoid colliding with the Newport pilot cutter *Belle Usk* causing her to strike the bullnose of the Lady Windsor lock entrance, damaging her forward starboard sponson; her sailings, however, were not affected. On Sunday 4 July she made the first 'public' post war call at Port Talbot on a return trip from Swansea and Porthcawl to Weston (The *Glen Gower* had called there, on charter, in 1948) and two days later, on Tuesday 6 July, the *Cardiff Queen* made the first post war trip to Tenby, from Swansea.

The *Glen Gower's* first trip to Boulogne, scheduled for Wednesday 14 July, was cancelled because of a gale but she was successful a week later on Wednesday 21 July. She sailed from the Railway Wharf at Newhaven at 09.36 with a mere 103 passengers. After a forty minute, mid-channel delay caused by steering trouble she arrived off Boulogne at 14.40 to find that the port was closed. A bucket dredger had picked up a magnetic mine in the harbour and, along with other shipping, the *Glen Gower* had to anchor in the roads until it was disposed of. She eventually arrived at her berth at 17.00 and left again at 18.17, arriving at Newhaven at 22.38.

Only a few days later further gales swept across southern England and caused the cancellation of four days sailings from Brighton. Similar conditions prevailed in the Bristol Channel

The Glen Gower *leaving the Royal Pier, Southampton, on Thursday 17 June 1954. Her day's work had started at 06.30 when she sailed light from Newhaven to Eastbourne. Having embarked her first passengers of the day, she left Eastbourne at 09.30; called at Brighton's Palace Pier at 10.26, and the West Pier at 10.40; then at Worthing at 11.30, arriving at Southampton at 14.50. Her departure from Southampton was at 16.30, arriving at the Palace Pier at 20.30, and Eastbourne at 22.05. She then anchored off Eastbourne for the night. (Her Worthing passengers disembarked at Brighton on the return journey, having been issued with a free rail ticket for their destination). The timetable for that day states 'Passengers will be able to view the Trans-Atlantic liners* Queen Elizabeth *and* United States *en route for New York.' The return fare from Brighton was 17/6d.* (Chris Collard Collection)

The Glen Usk *passing the Union Castle liner Llangibby Castle, arriving at Cashmore's yard on the River Usk for breaking up. Saturday 31 July 1954.* (Seaton Phillips)

causing, among other disruptions, the cancellation of the first post war sailing from Cardiff to Tenby, scheduled to be taken by the *Britannia.*

Luckily the weather improved in time for the August Bank Holiday weekend but one misfortune followed another. On Bank Holiday Monday 2 August the *Cardiff Queen* was scheduled to make a cruise along the Gower Coast to off Tenby. She left her berth at Swansea at 13.36 and while turning in the river, owing to a lack of water and a strong ebb tide, she sheered across the river and touched the bank with her rudder. Her starboard anchor was dropped and she stemmed the tide. In this position Capt. Gunn then skillfully manoeuvred her out of the river, between the breakwaters by 'dredging' her, ie. by letting her drift with the tide and checking her with the anchor as necessary. At 14.33 she hove up and proceeded, stern first, through the buoyed channel and into Swansea Bay where she anchored for an inspection of her steering gear. All visible parts were seen to be in good order so she proceeded on her cruise. Her Chief Officer, Mr Leslie Brook, recorded in the log that she was carrying an unusual amount of starboard helm. At 16.10 she turned off Port Eynon and at 16.40 the following message was sent, by morse lamp, to the coastguard station in Limeslade Bay:

> *Will you please ask agent to arrange for ship repairers representatives to meet vessel on arrival at Swansea as I think we have damaged rudder – Master.*

At 17.24 she anchored off the Outer Fairway Buoy and radioed to the Pilot Cutter *Roger Beck* for assistance up the river. She berthed at Pockett's Wharf at 19.10 where representatives of the Prince of Wales Dry Dock were waiting for her. On examination it was found necessary for her to be dry-docked for repairs. On the following morning the tug *Neath* assisted her to turn, towed her out of the river, slipped her tow at the Outer Fairway Buoy and then escorted the *Cardiff Queen*, at reduced speed, to Cardiff Roads where she assisted her to anchor to await the tide. She was later towed into the Mountstuart Dry Dock at Cardiff where she spent three days under repair. She was in trouble again on Tuesday 10 August when heavy seas, between Swansea and Ilfracombe, bent her forward starboard stanchions inboard breaking the wooden rail, demonstrating, not for the first time, her rather inferior sea-going qualities; the insufficient sheer of her hull causing her to dig her bows too deeply into the oncoming seas.

Despite these trials and tribulations the *Cardiff Queen* had made the first post-war landing call at Clovelly, from Swansea, on Thursday 10 June, and the *Bristol Queen* made the first post war trip from Cardiff to Tenby, via Ilfracombe, on Thursday 12 August, when she took over 1,000 passengers on a cruise from the 'Queen of the Welsh Watering Places', through Caldey Sound and along the Pembrokeshire coast towards the Elegug Stack Rocks.

During mid-August the *Britannia* developed recurring problems in her starboard paddle which led to her premature withdrawal from service after her sailings on Monday 23 August.

The *Glen Gower* had experienced a fair share of foul weather on the south coast and on the morning of Sunday 29 August, while leaving Worthing pier, the wind and tide set her down on an anchored dinghy in which two men were fishing. The dinghy sank, one man was picked up by another small boat and the other clambered aboard the *Glen Gower's* sponson. Both men were landed at the pier, little the worse for their experience.

The Glen Usk *at anchor off Lundy on Tuesday 31 August 1954. During the post-war years the* Glen Usk *was employed mainly on the Cardiff to Weston ferry, and her down-channel trips were the exception rather than the rule. On this particular day, however, she performed something of a marathon trip, which proved to be a little too much for her. She had sailed from Newport, Cardiff, Penarth, Barry and Ilfracombe, and arrived off Lundy at 15.30. Her return trip began at 17.43, half an hour late owing to a delay in embarking her passengers. Further time was then lost on her way up channel owing to her running short of coal and a consequent drop in steam pressure. She eventually arrived at Cardiff at 23.05, 1 hour and 25 minutes after she should have left for Newport. The trip was then terminated and the Newport passengers were returned to their destination by bus. Chief Officer David Miles's final remark in the log book entry for the day states: 'Finished at Cardiff. Lack of coal and time!'* (Seaton Phillips)

The beginning of September was relatively fine but all too soon a series of continuous depressions swept in from the south-west, causing widespread cancellations. The *Cardiff Queen* and *Bristol Queen* ran their last trips on Sunday 19 September and retired for the winter.

The *Glen Usk* took over the final two days sailings from Swansea which included a return trip to Ilfracombe, Clovelly and Lundy on Wednesday 22 September; she then returned up channel and on Sunday 26 September was scheduled for a day trip from Cardiff, Penarth and Barry to Ilfracombe. It was a particularly wild day as this extract from her log book shows:

> *Departed Barry Pier for Ilfracombe at 11.50 in a very strong WSW wind and heavy, confused seas. The vessel was steered WSW for Hurlestone Point in an effort to gain the lee of the land and smoother water. As the vessel began to open out Nash Point the seas became increasingly high, dangerous and powerful, necessitating the use of the engines in order that the vessel could meet them. Despite these precautions, three high and dangerous seas successively struck the vessel on the bluff of the starboard bow, shredded to ribbons the canvas weather cloth, lifted both bow anchors out of the deck, unshipped and carried aft the vessel's mooring ropes and forcefully drove the six buoyant seats from the foredeck hard against the fore part of the chartroom. No passengers suffered injury because the master, five minutes before, had ordered all people from the foredeck, at the same time roping the area off. The master then considered it prudent to put the vessel before the sea, bringing her around with difficulty. At 12.35 the vessel was about and proceeding to Barry for shelter.*

Sunday 26 September marked the eighth day of cancellations that month on the south coast, bringing the total loss of sailing days for the *Glen Gower's* season to twenty five. The Boulogne trips in particular had been very badly affected; out of ten scheduled trips one was cancelled because of 'insufficient crew' and three were lost because of gales. The four which took place were so poorly patronised, carrying an average of only 135 passengers per trip, that the final two crossings were cancelled in advance and other sailings were substituted. The Chairman, however, stated:

> *While the full co-operation of the Railway Executive in the matter of special trains to Newhaven was secured these trips were run at a heavy loss... The company's experience at any rate established the fact beyond doubt that the ordinary citizen when on holiday does not favour having to go to a commercial port to make a day trip and certainly does not go away armed with a passport. The only comfort which can be taken from this experience is that had the facilities offered not been tested it would not have been possible for us to fully substantiate our continuing arguments and requests to the Government.*

The *Glen Gower* left Newhaven and Brighton on the morning of Monday 27 September and arrived at Bristol at 21.30 on the following day. She then ran in the Bristol Channel until making her last trips on Sunday 3 October. The *Ravenswood* had retired for the winter on Sunday 26 September and the *Glen Usk* closed the season, rather later than usual, on Monday 18 October, her master, Capt. Findlay Brander, retiring after thirty-three years with the company.

What a season it had been. The annual statement by the Chairman made, in part, depressing reading:

> *It is very disappointing to me year after year to have to make continual complaints about the bad weather which now appears to characterise the English summer and which is so crippling to the efforts which are being made to make the company's business a success. The unfortunate fact remains, however, that of five successive stormy summers 1954 proved to be quite the worst. I think it speaks well for the management and employees of the company that their enthusiasm and optimism remains undiminished in spite of what many people are beginning to regard as an alteration in the summer weather normally enjoyed by these islands.*

At the directors meeting on Wednesday 20 October 1954 it was announced that the bank's accountants were to visit Bristol to investigate the company's position; the matter of an overdraft would receive their attention after they had inspected the accountant's reports. The company's trading loss for the 1954 season amounted to just over £48,000 In addition, no depreciation had been charged on the steamers for a number of years and their value stood at an unrealistically high figure on the balance sheet. This was rectified by charging £108,000 depreciation which brought the total deficit on the profit and loss account to over £155,000.

In November an overdraft of £150,000 was arranged and an executive committee of three members, including Mr Smith-Cox, was set up with power to act on behalf of the board in accordance with the requirements of the Westminster Bank. A financial controller was appointed, Mr W. Walker of Messrs Latham & Co., as representative of the bank. The Chaiman's statement continued:

> *Your Directors are now satisfied that a start has been made upon the major operation of modernising the administration and outlook of the company. Whereas we hardly expected any beneficial results from the innovations effected to be shown to any great extent in 1954, I cannot deny that the adverse season was a cruel blow and might well have been a fatal one but for the goodwill of the company's bankers.*

Throughout the year plans for the reconstruction of Minehead Pier had continued. Discussions had taken place between the company, the Consultant Engineers Lewis, Gregory & Co. and the Ministry of Works and at the board meeting on Thursday 26 August 1954 there was mention of an 'alternative design' having been proposed. Mr John MacGregor, the company's Works Manager, agreed with the proposals 'subject to the overall length and number of landings being the same as the original pier.' However, in view of the company's financial situation at the end of the year the matter was deferred until a later date.

Throughout the season the *Empress Queen* in deteriorating condition, remained laid up at Narrow Quay, Bristol, costing the company between £3,000 and £6,000 per year in standing charges. In January 1954 the agents Messrs C.W. Kellock & Co. were negotiating with a prospective Greek purchaser, John Toyas, and the board agreed to accept his offer of £70,000 for her, but by the end of March 1954 negotiations had fallen through. Further enquiries were made by a German company and also by Coast Lines Ltd, all of which came to nothing. By October the purchase price had been reduced to £43,000 and by February 1955 several offers had been received to buy her for scrap, the highest being £19,000 all of which had been refused. Kellock's then received an offer of £30,000 from a Greek company who were agreeable to paying up to £1,000 for a dockside trial; the offer was accepted.

On Monday 7 March 1955, with Capt. Gunn in command, the *Empress Queen* was moved from Narrow Quay to the Floating Harbour where steam was raised in readiness for her engine trials which took place in the Cumberland Basin on Saturday 12 March. From the following Tuesday until Thursday 24 March she was in Hill's dry dock for inspection. The prospective purchasers were satisfied with her performance and condition and the details of the sale were completed on Friday 1 April.

Her new owners were the Kavounides Shipping Company of Athens. While Capt. Nicholas Kavounides, one of the three principals of the company – all were brothers – was negotiating in Bristol, another was making a tour of Italian shipyards to see how quickly and economically her accommodation could be converted for her intended role. It was proposed to run her on ten-day and fourteen-day cruises in the Mediterranean as well as cruises from her home port of Piraeus to the Greek islands.

Shortly before leaving Bristol on Sunday 3 April 1955 her new owners held a service on board, in front of an improvised altar, while the company's flag was hoisted and the new name was blessed. She had been renamed *Philippos* by the brothers, in memory of their late father, the founder of the company. Her funnel, with the cowl removed, was painted salmon pink with a narrow black top. In heavy rain, flying the Greek national flag, she left the Cumberland Basin at 15.30 in tow of the tugs *John King* and *Volunteer*. She rounded the Horseshoe Bend at 16.20, slipped her tow off Avonmouth, landed her compass adjuster at Barry at about 20.00 and set off for Falmouth to take on fuel. Her next scheduled stop for bunkering was at Corunna in Spain and the whole journey to Piraeus was expected to take nine days. In fact, owing to delays caused by bad weather, it took nearly three weeks.

The *Empress Queen's* career in the Bristol Channel and on the south coast had not been a success: the no-passport cross channel trips for which she had been intended were still prohibited and she had been found unsuitable for coastal cruising. She was, however, a fine

The Empress Queen *in the Cumberland basin, on the morning of Saturday 12 March 1955, undergoing engine trials for the Kavounides brothers.* (Edwin Keen)

The Departure Of The *Philippos*, Sunday 3 April 1955.

Leaving the Cumberland Basin and entering the lock. (H.G. Owen Collection)

At 15.30 the Philippos *passes Hotwells Landing Stage for the last time, on her journey to Greece. Refuelling stops and bad weather extended the anticipated duration of the voyage by over a week. After leaving Falmouth on 6 April she arrived in Corunna two days later. She then sailed on 9 April and called at Lisbon on 11 April; Gibraltar on 12 April; Algiers on 14 April, and Bona on 15 April, before arriving at Piraeus on Wednesday 20 April.* (John Brown Collection)

Heading down the Avon Gorge. The tugs John King, *(ahead), and* Volunteer, *(astern), perform, for the last time, a duty which was familiar to them from years past. They were often used to assist the* Empress Queen *on her passages up and down the River Avon.* (Edwin Keen)

Rounding the Horseshoe Bend. (H.G. Owen Collection)

ship and although her UK years came to a sad end she was destined for a brighter and more successful future in Greek waters.

After her initial alterations she began a timetable of cruises around the islands of the Cyclades and Dodecanese in the summer of 1955. This service continued until early 1959 when her owners commissioned the Alisa Shipbuilding Co. to draw up further plans for alterations to her accommodation. At the same time she was re-engined; her original, twenty knot turbines being replaced by two Crossley diesels which gave her a much reduced, but much more economical speed of about sixteen knots. She resumed service in the summer of 1959, this time running cruises to Brindisi and Venice, and also from Piraeus to Mykonos and Rhodes. The 1960s were her halcyon years but disaster struck in the early 1970s. On 23 February 1972, while undergoing maintenance and repair work, fire broke out on one of her lower decks. Tugs towed her clear of other shipping, but despite strenuous efforts the fire spread rapidly and could not be controlled. The inferno raged throughout the ship and eventually burned itself out, leaving a virtually empty and twisted hulk, totally beyond repair. The ill-fortune which had haunted her early career had never entirely left her and led to her untimely end after only thirty-two years in service.

Shortly after the departure of the *Philippos* in March 1955, by a most ironic twist of fate, developments began taking place with regard to the cross-channel trips. At the management committee's meeting on Friday 17 September 1954 the south coast services had been discussed in detail, as well as the prospects of no-passport trips in 1955, but as there appeared to be little hope of that facility being granted it was unanimously agreed that the company should abandon the south coast services entirely. It was also agreed that as the chairman had written to Sir Walter Monckton MP, regarding no-passport facilities, the company should delay informing the south coast pier authorities of this decision until a later date, pending Sir Walter's reply. This was received in November 1954 in which he stated that there was no possibility of no-passport trips to France in the near future.

This letter appears to have instigated considerable activity in an effort to bring matters to a more favourable conclusion. On Tuesday 16 November questions were asked in the House of Commons: the MP for Brighton (Pavilion), Mr W. Teeling, asked the President of the Board of Trade, Mr Peter Thorneycroft, if he would consult with the Home Office and other departments concerned 'with a view to the relaxation of the present passport requirements which hinder day cruises to Continental coastal towns.' The President replied that he was in consultation with the other ministers concerned. Mr Teeling then stated that unless such obstacles were removed P&A Campbell Ltd would be forced to withdraw their south coast services entirely and asked if he would allow a deputation of Town Clerks and MPs from the south coast to discuss the matter with him. At the board meeting on Wednesday 16 February 1955 it was reported that the deputation and Government officials had met and that there was 'a good possibility of no-passport trips'.

Company representatives met with the Home Secretary on Friday March 1955 and the continuing negotiations attracted the attention of the national press when, on Monday 21 March, the *Daily Express* reported that Foreign Office, Immigration and Customs officials were visiting Eastbourne pier to inspect the facilities for the embarking and disembarking of cross channel passengers.

At the board meeting on Thursday 19 May it was stated that provisional arrangements had been made and two days later the *Bristol Evening Post* printed the following article:

A Home Office statement issued today says 'British and French Government representatives who met in London on May 19 and 20 reached complete agreement on the subject of no-passport day excursions between the two countries.

The agreement covers the period between June 17 and September 30 and is to be reviewed after October 1. Excursions from England will be allowed from Southend, Gravesend, Folkestone, Eastbourne and Newhaven.

The passengers must be British subjects, (or citizens of the Irish Republic) and will have to furnish three passport type photographs and complete a four part card bearing prescribed particulars.

The cards will be issued by the shipping companies on the day of sailing, French excursionists coming here will complete a somewhat similar card and carry their national identity cards.'

At last, after years of patient endeavour, the company had achieved its goal. A share of good fortune was long overdue and this came in 1955, not only with the resumption of no-passport trips but in the best possible form – a good summer!

The *Glen Usk* and *Glen Gower* were in service for the very fine Easter weekend. The latter took over 750 passengers on a cruise from Newport to Bristol on Easter Sunday 10 April and a similar number to Ilfracombe on the following day before re-entering the Bristol City Docks on Thursday 14 April leaving the *Glen Usk*, now under the command of Capt. Leo Virgo, to maintain the Cardiff to Weston ferry.

On the morning of Thursday 21 April the *Ravenswood* was moved from the Merchants Dock to Hill's Dry Dock for her five-yearly Board of Trade survey. At the board meeting on Thursday 19 May a report was submitted on the condition of her hull and of the major renewals required;

The Glen Gower *at the Pier Head, Cardiff, during her Easter sailings in 1955.* (Viv Davies)

The Glen Usk *turning on an ebb tide at Newport in 1955; a manoeuvre whereby the steamer was held close to the landing stage by only her stern rope, while she moved slowly forward, upstream into the flow of the tide. When her bow had swung around sufficiently for her to head downstream, the stern rope was cast off.* (Lionel Vaughan)

twenty-two plates needed replacement at an estimated cost of £12,000. In view of her age and the company's financial position it was felt that there was no alternative other than to dispose of her, the financial controller confirming that the bank would not provide the money for such repairs. She was accordingly laid up in the Merchants Dock and advertised for sale.

At the same meeting it was decided that plans for the reconstruction of Minehead pier should be 'held over for the time being' and also that an investigation should be carried out regarding the income and expenditure of the Underfall Yard after the winter overhaul of the last steamer had been completed.

The *Bristol Queen* entered service on Thursday 26 May – General Election day. That evening she left Hotwells, complete with a small orchestra – 'The White Funnel Players' – for an 'Election Cruise' down channel, during which the election results were broadcast as they were received. It was a novel idea but the evening was extremely wet and only about 300 passengers were aboard.

After the completion of extensive work on her paddle wheels, the *Britannia* entered service on Sunday 19 June, allowing the *Glen Gower*, which had re-entered service in late May, to leave for the south coast on Monday 20 June.

The first no-passport trip took place on Thursday 23 June 1955 amid a blaze of publicity. The *Western Daily Press* stated:

> *The fully booked sailing to Boulogne from Newhaven at 09.15 and Eastbourne at 11.00 will be a gala event of Anglo-French goodwill and general festivity with civic celebrations ashore in France.*

The Glen Gower *at Boulogne on the first post-war, No Passport trip to France, Thursday 23 June 1955.* (Gordon Wood)

> *Celebrities aboard the flag bedecked* Glen Gower *will include film and stage stars and added gaiety will be provided by music from the steamer's shipboard band, the White Funnel Players...*

The lifting of passport restrictions and the calls at Eastbourne pier made a considerable difference to passenger figures: on the first eight trips the average number of passengers carried from Newhaven was a mere thirty-one, but from Eastbourne the figure was 382.

The innovations and improvements of 1954 had been further extended and a Publicity Manager had been appointed at the beginning of the year. Music and entertainment became a feature of many trips and some of the performers went on to international fame and stardom; Shirley Bassey, for example, appeared on several of the 'Showboat' cruises. Miss Bassey was then at a very early stage in her career but it was apparent to all who saw her, often performing under adverse weather conditions, that she was destined for the glittering future which she still enjoys.

Although the weather in June was variable a long, hot, dry spell began in early July and the steamers were packed to capacity on many occasions. The *Cardiff Queen*, for instance, ran a cruise from Newport to Bristol on the afternoon of Sunday 31 July taking her maxium 1,107 passengers and leaving many behind. On the following day, however, she developed boiler trouble for the second time that season and spent a few days in Bristol under repair. She was back in service in time to run the first post-war trip to Milford Haven, from Swansea and Ilfracombe, on Sunday 8 August. This took place in conjunction with a visit of Her Majesty the Queen in the Royal Yacht *Britannia* but, despite the fine weather, the trip was poorly patronised, only 146 passengers making the cruise from Milford around the Royal Yacht and her escorts.

On Friday 19 August the *Glen Usk* met with a most unfortunate accident at Newport: the logbook gives the details:

> *On approaching the pontoon at 23.20, approx. two hours ebb at Bristol, the vessel was positioned for an ebb swing. Because of the failure to land the heaving line, to which was attached the 6in swinging rope, the vessel was caught by the ebb tide and commenced to drift down the river, bow towards left bank. Port anchor prepared for use but before it could be let go the vessel's rudder touched the river bank, held fast in the mud and the vessel swung upon it bow down the river. The vessel again swung when the ebb tide caught the port quarter, laying her across the river. The vessel was then backed away from the bank and the port anchor was let go. The vessel was brought up and positioned for taking the pontoon lying bow up and starboard side to. The anchor was hove up. After landing 90 passengers the vessel was swung on the pontoon and proceeded to anchorage in Cardiff Roads. While on passage down river it was discovered that on account of the abnormal amount of helm carried the rudder had sustained damage. The rudder was examined in Cardiff Roads and was found to be fifteen to twenty degrees out of line, being set to port. The master informed Burnham Radio who passed the message to the Works Manager and Traffic Manager. Time 01.00, Saturday 20 August 1955.*

She entered dry dock at Avonmouth later that day for repairs and was back in service on Tuesday 23 August. The *Bristol Queen* replaced her on the ferry, while the *Britannia* maintained the Bristol and Cardiff to Ilfracombe trips.

The *Cardiff Queen* once again missed a few days sailings towards the end of August because of boiler trouble. Owing to the persistent nature of the defect – fractured tubes – representatives of her builders were called in to investigate, but it was Campbells' Marine Superintendent, John MacGregor, who diagnosed the source of the problem – her lying on the mud at Swansea at low tide; the slight hogging and sagging as she took to the ground and on refloating 'worked' the boilers, causing the tubes to fracture. He discovered it by bolting a bar between the boiler seats and later finding that the bolts were bent. The remedy suggested was the fitting of strengthening pieces to the boiler seatings. The repairs were to be effected during the following winter but as a temporary measure, until the end of the season she was kept afloat at all times by anchoring in Swansea Bay overnight when necessary and spending her off service days in the Prince of Wales Dock. She was due to retire for the winter and actually moored at the Underfall Yard on Wednesday 14 September, but on the following Friday the *Britannia* developed paddle trouble and had to finish her season earlier than scheduled. Consequently the *Cardiff Queen* re-entered service to replace her on Saturday 17 September and ran for a further ten days.

The final trip to Ilfracombe, from Cardiff, took place on Sunday 2 October. The outward journey was taken by the *Glen Usk*, which returned to Cardiff inmdiately after landing her passengers and the return trip was taken by the *Glen Gower*, on the last lap of her homeward journey from Brighton. The season was eventually closed by the *Glen Usk* on Monday 10 October 1955.

The *Ravenswood* had spent the season laid up in the Merchants Dock, Bristol and was eventually sold for scrap to the British Iron & Steel Corporation for £3,300. With Capt. Jack George on her bridge she was towed down the Avon by the tugs *John Payne* and *Sea Prince*, early on the morning of Thursday 20 October, to off Avonmouth where a Newport tug was waiting to take her across the channel. Having arrived too late to make the berth on the falling tide she was taken into the Alexandra Dock, Newport, until the following morning when when she was towed up the River Usk to her final resting place at John Cashmore's yard.

With her demise went a significant part of White Funnel Fleet history. She was the first steamer built specifically for Campbells' Bristol Channel trade and which, under the command of Capt. Alec Campbell, took part in the spirited races against Edwards, Robertson's *Lorna Doone* and her infamous commander, Capt. 'Satan' Hucker. The *Ravenswood* was a regular visitor to all the Bristol Channel resorts before venturing on to the south coast in 1912. She served in the First World War, and a few years after resuming her peace-time duties she reopened the sailings from Brighton in company with the *Devonia* and *Brighton Belle* in 1923. After operating in the Bristol Channel from 1926 to 1940 she again flew the White Ensign from 1941 to 1945. During the years following the Second World War she was confined to maintaining the shorter trips in the upper reaches of the Bristol Channel. Towards the end of her career she began to run rather erratically, her slow speed led to poor timekeeping and her age was beginning to take its toll, but after sixty-four years of service to both her company and her country she was long overdue for retirement.

The Chairman's annual statement to shareholders, reviewing the 1955 season, contained a wealth of information: it is quoted here in slightly edited form:

At last year's Annual General Meeting I could say little that was encouraging but I did express the hope that the innovations explained in some detail in my circulated statement, coupled with a fine summer, might enable our services to regain their popular appeal. The weather in 1955 was good, the majority of the innovations proved to be successful and as a result the trading loss of £48,102 of 1954 has been turned into a trading profit of £26,656 in 1955.

Two other features of the accounts merit special mention. It will be observed that a further sum of £6,084 has been provided for depreciation, the effect of which is that after making the necessary adjustments covering the sales of the 'Empress Queen' *and the* 'Ravenswood', *the present net value of the five steamers now comprising the White Funnel Fleet stands at £120,000. It will also be observed that £10,000 has been reserved as 'provision for special repairs.' Shareholders may be aware that in order to retain her passenger certificates each steamer is subjected to an official quinquennial survey. On the basis of data gained from the latest survey of the* 'Glen Usk' *– an excellent vessel from an operational point of view, but one no longer young – it has been deemed prudent to reserve this amount mainly in respect of the next quinquennial survey of the* 'Britannia' *which is due in 1957.*

The Board are doubtful whether any profit would have been made in 1955 had not the Company's outlook and methods been radically revised... High and increasing costs affect almost every branch of the Company's activities and to give shareholders a practical idea of this I may say that our costs are now some four or five times higher than they were in 1922 and that it cost approximately £70,000 more to run five steamers in 1955 than it cost to run seven in 1947. In order to offset this, fares were increased in 1955 and have been further increased for 1956, but it is obvious that there are limits to what can be done in this direction, particularly at a time when the company is facing intensive competition from other sources of entertainment and means of transport and is seeking to re-establish its popularity with the public and particularly with the younger generation. Even now fares are little more than double the 1922 fares. It is clear therefore that if the present services are to continue, the only answer is to increase the number of passengers carried per steamer and I am glad to be able to say that in 1955 the average per steamer was in excess of any previous figure. The numbers carried on excursions from Ilfracombe were the highest since 1924, when eight steamers were operating in the Bristol Channel, and the numbers carried from Swansea were double those of 1954 and equal to those of the best pre-war years... On the Cardiff to Weston service the 1954 figures of total passengers carried were exceeded by 40,000 in each direction...

With regard to the 'no-passport' trips between Newhaven, Eastbourne and Boulogne, I may say that the board takes some satisfaction in knowing that it was their efforts which pioneered this concession not only for this company but for other passenger steamer proprietors. The service proved to be an unqualified success, the administrative difficulties forecasted in some quarters were not present in practice and some 16,000 passengers were carried on the thirty-seven trips, with none cancelled. Despite the fears expressed in some quarters the concession was not abused and as a result no-passport facilities will, in 1956, be available from Brighton, Eastbourne and Hastings, as in the pre-war years. The number of crossings scheduled for next season is in consequence nearly twice the number for 1955.

The 1956 season began well. Good Friday fell on 30 March and for the third successive Easter both the *Glen Usk*, (Capt. L. Virgo) and *Glen Gower*, (Capt. J. W. Harris) were in service, following a pattern of sailings similar to that of the previous two years. The *Glen Gower* had

The Ravenswood *on her arrival at the breakers yard on the morning of Friday 21 October 1955. The decision to withdraw the* Ravenswood *from service, following her survey in May 1955, meant that considerable modifications had to be made to the sailing plans for that season. Among the trips which were abandoned was a proposed Cardiff-Ilfracombe-Bideford sailing by the* Ravenswood. *She was then to be based, experimentally, at Bideford and Ilfracombe for a few days, with one or two sailings to Lundy, before returning to Cardiff.* (John Brown Collection)

The Ravenswood's *demolition under way. Saturday 29 October 1955.* (John Brown)

been fitted with radar during the winter, the apparatus having been removed from the *Empress Queen* early in 1954, and held in storage.

In mid-April three of the steamers earned a very welcome £500 revenue without leaving the harbour. The Queen and the Duke of Edinburgh paid a visit to Bristol which included a tour of the City Docks in the Royal Barge. The *Bristol Queen*, at the Mardyke Wharf, the *Cardiff Queen*, at the Wapping Wharf and the *Glen Gower*, at the City Centre, were used as 'Grandstands' for spectators. The log of the *Glen Gower* records:

Tuesday 17 April 1956
08.30 Passengers boarded.
11.27 Dipped Ensign in salute to HM The Queen
13.00 Vessel cleared of passengers

The deployment of the steamers was similar to that of the previous year. The *Glen Gower* left Cardiff for the south coast on Wednesday 16 May and made her first crossing to Boulogne on Whit Sunday 20 May, via Brighton, Eastbourne and Hastings.

The *Bristol Queen*, with Capt. George, and the *Cardiff Queen*, with Capt. Gunn, both entered service on Friday 18 May. The *Cardiff Queen*, after compass adjusting in Barry Roads, then made the first post-war call at the newly renovated Mumbles Pier. Although both the *Cardiff Queen* and *Bristol Queen* then made several calls, it was the latter which had the honour of attending the official re-opening ceremony on the afternoon of Saturday 9 June 1956.

The Bristol Queen *leaving Mumbles, for a cruise along the Gower coast, following the official re-opening of the pier, Saturday 9 June 1956.* (Lionel Vaughan Collection)

At the end of May and early June the *Bristol Queen* was experiencing boiler trouble which necessitated her visiting the Underfall Yard for several days for repairs. At about the same time the *Glen Usk* developed paddle trouble, the *Britannia* was therefore brought into service earlier than intended, on Thursday 7 June, to avoid any cancellations.

Music and Entertainment were once again a feature of many of the sailings and included jazz cruises, beauty contests and cabaret-style 'Showboats'. The artists, often having to perform under adverse weather conditions, displayed a wide variety of talents and ranged from the 'Pin-up' personality Sabrina to the Malayan Police Pipe and Drum Band!

BBC Television provided some good publicity when one of the 'Saturday Night Out' series of programmes featured Weston Super Mare. During the broadcast the *Cardiff Queen* arrived at Birnbeck pier and Capt. Gunn was interviewed by Brian Johnston before she sailed. History was made in the closing part of the programme with the first live air to ground transmission in the BBC's West region. Raymond Baxter was the commentator in one of two Westland helicopters; the other, carrying the camera, provided some spectacular views of the *Cardiff Queen* making her way across the channel.

The entertainment and extra publicity no doubt attracted an additional number of passengers but as the season progressed it proved to be one of shocking weather, wet and unsettled conditions being all too common. Passenger figures, overall, fell and caused considerable concern within the company, the directors continually discussing ways of alleviating the inevitable trading loss.

Thursday 26 July 1956 was a day of surprises. The international news was dominated by the Middle East when Egypt's President Nasser announced the nationalisation of the Anglo-French owned Suez Canal. Closer to home, on a more modest scale perhaps but no less startling was the announcement that P&A Campbell Ltd were to transfer their headquarters from Bristol to Cardiff. A newspaper article, with the headline 'Campbell's will move to Cardiff. City's poor support', stated,

> *P&A Campbell, who have been sending their steamers from Bristol since 1887, are transferring their business to Cardiff next year. This surprise announcement was made before a meeting of shareholders at the Grand Hotel today by Mr A. Roy Boucher, chairman of the company.*

He told the *Evening World* afterwards:

> *I know that this will come as a big shock for Bristol but we must think of the company's financial position. We will save a lot of money by moving to Cardiff...*
>
> *I must emphasise that we have no quarrel with Bristol or the Port of Bristol Authority but I cannot help being disappointed with the small number of people we take from Bristol. It is a sad fact that we carry twelve people from Wales for every one from Bristol.*
>
> *It is a costly business making the long journey down the river and to carry on here would be expensive in overheads. I understand that all the facilities we need for our ships are available to us in Cardiff.*

At the end of July and in early August gales disrupted sailings. On Sunday 29 July the *Bristol Queen* curtailed her trip to Ilfracombe at Barry because of exceptionally heavy seas, even in the upper reaches of the channel. On the following day the *Britannia's* trip from Ilfracombe to Clovelly was cancelled for the same reason: this was a most unusual occurrence for Capt. Murphy, a master who usually pressed on regardless of the weather!

On the morning of Saturday 18 August the *Bristol Queen* crossed from Cardiff to Weston in gale force winds but was unable to berth at the pier after four attempts. She crossed the channel to Barry where the *Britannia*, stormbound on a trip from Avonmouth to Ilfracombe, embarked the *Bristol Queen's* passengers and took over her ferry sailings for the rest of the day. The *Britannia* offered much less wind resistance and was consequently, somewhat easier to berth at Birnbeck Pier in the prevailing conditions

During that night the gale abated and on the following morning, Sunday 19 August, the *Bristol Queen* proceeded on her scheduled down-channel trip. She left Ilfracombe at 13.42 and was bound for Tenby when, at 14.25, a loud bang and rumbling sound were heard in the port paddle wheel. She was stopped immediately and an inspection revealed that one of the star centre pins had broken off, carrying with it a driving arm and radius rod. A radio message was sent to the *Cardiff Queen* for assistance. She had sailed from Ilfracombe for Porthcawl and Mumbles at 14.15 and about 45 minutes later reached the *Bristol Queen's* position, recorded in the log with Capt. George's usual precision as 'Lat. 51 degrees 20' 30" North, Long. 4 degrees 16' 30" West. Capstone Hill bearing SE x S¼S, 9.5 miles'. Both ships were rolling heavily in the swell but after skillful manoeuvring by Capt. Gunn his crew succeded in reaching the *Bristol Queen* with a tow rope. At 15.35 the tow commenced with the *Bristol Queen's* engines being kept in the 'Dead slow astern' position to prevent the paddles turning and causing further damage. At 19.35 the two ships arrived in Swansea Bay where the *Bristol Queen* dropped anchor. The towing distance was twenty-one nautical miles which had taken exactly four hours at a speed of 5.25 knots. The *Cardiff Queen* slipped her tow and proceeded to run her scheduled evening cruise from Mumbles to Ilfracombe.

The *Bristol Queen* was then taken in tow by the tugs *Waterloo* and *Alexandra* and berthed in the Prince of Wales Dock, Swansea, at 21.30. She left Swansea for the long haul to Bristol in tow of the tugs *Langland* and *Alexandra* on the evening of Monday 20 August, clearing the breakwater at 18.23. The log continues:

Tuesday 21 August 1956.

02.26 *Nash Light abeam.*
04.09 *Bristol pilot boarded tug off Barry.*
07.17 *Anchored in Walton Bay.*
17.30 Langland *made fast and proceeded.*
20.03 *Moored Cumberland Basin.*
21.25 *Moored at Hill's Dockyard.*

Repairs commenced on the following day and she was back in service from Saturday 25 August. After running her final trips on Wednesday 12 September she was kept in steam at Bristol until the following week, during which time she was loaded with furniture, equipment and stationery etc. from the office at Britannia Buildings to be transferred to the new premises across the channel. She sailed from the Cumberland Basin at 06.30 on Monday 17 September for the Pier

With his vessel out of action following her paddle damage, Capt. George takes the wheel of the Bristol Queen *as the* Cardiff Queen *begins towing her across the channel to Swansea. No doubt Capt. George wanted to 'get the feel' of his ship under tow before handing over to the helmsmen, Sunday 19 August 1956.* (John Brown Collection)

Head, Cardiff where she was unloaded during the course of the day, entering Penarth Dock that evening; the first of the steamers to occupy the company's new winter quarters.

The season was drawing to its close and was destined to end in some confusion. It was anticipated that the five-yearly survey of the *Britannia* would reveal the need for repairs and replacements costing more than the £10,000 already set aside for that purpose. As the company's deteriorating financial situation would render such possible expenditure untenable, she was to be laid up and held in 'strategic reserve'. Accordingly her final sailing was to be a 'Farewell Cruise' scheduled for Wednesday 19 September.

It was a day trip from Bristol and Clevedon to Ilfracombe, limited to 250 passengers, at a cost of two guineas including a 'Fourchette Luncheon' and light tea. On that morning she moored at Hotwells at 08.00 when she was boarded by the Lord Mayor of Bristol and guests. After several speeches she sailed at 08.45, called at Clevedon where she was visited by the Chairman of the Urban District Council and other local dignitaries, before sailing direct to Ilfracombe. Shortly after her arrival at 12.45 the new Bristol Britannia aircraft flew low overhead in salute. Her return sailing at 16.05 was preceded by more nostalgic speeches, during which Capt. Murphy was presented with a commemorative silver cup. She arrived at Hotwells at 20.20 and sailed almost immediately for Cardiff in readiness to enter Penarth Dock on Thursday 20 September.

However, early that morning the *Glen Usk* lying overnight at Newport, was found to have a badly leaking boiler. The Engineering Superintendent and Traffic Manager were informed and, in consequence, she was directed to Penarth Dock to lay up.

The *Britannia*, therefore, remained in service and took over the ferry sailings from the *Glen Usk* for a further week until entering Penarth Dock on Thursday 27 September. Capt. Murphy's final entry made on the last page of the *Britannia's* log book was the single word – 'Finis'!

The *Glen Gower* completed her disastrous south coast season on Monday 24 September, having lost the equivalent of about four weeks sailings partly because of boiler trouble but mainly because of the bad weather. The Boulogne trips had been particularly badly affected; 12,000 passengers had been carried from four ports, with twelve cancellations, in 1956 as against 16,000 from two ports, with no cancellations, in 1955. She arrived at Cardiff on the evening of Wednesday 26 September after an uneventful but slow round trip, taking twenty-six hours from Brighton to Ilfracombe. She then took over the ferry sailings from the *Britannia* until closing the season on Monday 13 October. On the following day she arrived at Bristol and moored at the Mardyke Wharf, the solitary White Funnel steamer in the Floating Harbour that winter.

At the two board meetings in October 1956 there were many matters to be discussed, including the official approval of the move to Cardiff. The new offices, at 4, Dock Chambers, Bute Street, were to be rented at a cost of £275 per year. The sale of the premises at 1 and 2 Britannia Buildings, Bristol, realised £3,250; No.3 Britannia Buildings being retained as a store room and enquiry office. The Underfall Yard of Campbell & Banks was sold to Charles Hill & Son Ltd, with goodwill and assets, for £5,500 including some tools, machinery and equipment. The remaining apparatus was later sold by auction.

The trading loss for 1956 amounted to just over £56,000. A meeting with bank representatives revealed that they were anxious for the company to continue operating and were

Surely one of the most dramatic photographs of a White Funnel steamer in the post-war years. Despite nearing the end of her career the Britannia *had a good turn of speed to the last. She is seen here storming out of Ilfracombe, at full speed, on Bank Holiday Monday 6 August 1956, taking her passengers on a cruise to Bideford Bay. It was said of her master, Capt. Albert Murphy, that he knew only three engine room telegraph positions – Full Ahead, Full Astern and Stop. Norman Bird states, 'Mr Smith-Cox's punishing, unrealistic schedules and insistence on trying to maintain punctuality, combined with Capt. Murphy's sportsmanship were a powerful combination." However, everyone agreed that it was fitting that the* Britannia's *final years should be under the command of such a consummate seaman and expert ship handler.* (Phillip Tolley)

The *Britannia's* 'Farewell Cruise'.

Leaving Bristol at 08.45 on Wednesday 19 September 1956. (Edwin Keen)

Rounding the Horseshoe Bend in the River Avon. (H.G. Owen)

Steaming down channel. (H.G. Owen)

The Britannia*'s identification flags, (from top to bottom), GFNP, fly from her foremast. The black funnel cowls were a distinctive feature of the Campbell steamers. They were correctly called 'watersheds' and their prime function was to prevent rain and salt spray from entering the space between the inner and outer funnel casings and causing rust. They also prevented the unsightly smoke-blackening of the tops of their plain white funnels. Although usually referred to as cowls, they were also known as 'caps', 'navy or naval tops', (after the fashion of warships), and among the older P&A Campbell personnel as 'bonnets'.* (H.G. Owen)

The Britannia *waits to embark her final passengers at Ilfracombe Pier for the return trip to Clevedon and Bristol.* (H.G. Owen)

At 16.00 Captain Murphy, at the telegraphs, gives the order to let go as he and Chief Officer William Watson prepare to take the Britannia *out of Ilfracombe for the last time.* (H.G. Owen)

Having discharged her passengers at Bristol at the end of her Farewell Cruise, the Britannia *swings on the ebb tide to return to Cardiff.* (Lionel Vaughan collection)

The Britannia *in Penarth Dock, Saturday 1 December 1956.* (John Brown)

The Britannia *at her final resting place at Cashmore's yard, Newport, on Friday 7 December 1956.* (Chris Collard Collection)

The Britannia's *demolition under way on Sunday 30 December 1956. Her 1947 boiler and its close proximity to the deckhead can clearly be seen.* (John Brown)

prepared to maintain an overdraft but only on condition that the south coast services were terminated; that the *Britannia* was disposed of; and that a reduction in the number of employees should be made where possible. Accordingly Capts. A.V. Murphy, W.F. Watson and J.A. Harris left the company towards the end of the year.

The *Britannia's* 'strategic reserve' was therefore short lived. She was advertised for sale and was purchased, in November, by the British Iron & Steel Corporation for £13,000. Early on the cold and foggy morning of Friday 7 December two Cardiff tugs towed her from Penarth Dock on her last journey to the breakers yard at Newport.

Launched sixty years before, the *Britannia* was the third of a famous trio of steamers, and all the experience gained in the building and running of her two predecessors, the *Westward Ho* and the *Cambria,* went into the *Britannia.* She was renowned for her speed, manoeuvrability and seaworthiness. As Flagship of the fleet from 1896 to 1946 she was commanded originally by Capt. Peter Campbell and later by the company's senior masters – Capt. Daniel Taylor and Capt. Jack George. After the re-boilering and re-building of 1947 she was never quite the same again; the new boiler made her heavy on fuel and subsequently led to her running for short seasons. The paddle troubles of the last few years added to her problems but she was an incomparable ship to the end; without doubt one of the finest examples of paddle steamer design and construction.

The Glen Usk *and* Bristol Queen *in Penarth Dock, 22 September 1956.* (Edwin Keen)

1957/1959 – Taxing Times

The bleakest period in the history of P&A Campbell Ltd began in 1957. Over the following few years drastic steps were to be taken to check the company's decline and near demise. In addition to the measures already outlined at the end of 1956 it was proposed that three steamers should operate during the forthcoming season: the *Bristol Queen* on the Bristol or Cardiff – down channel route, the *Glen Gower* on the ferry, and the *Cardiff Queen* on the Swansea service. The *Glen Usk* would remain in Penarth Dock, and after repairs to her boiler, would be held in reserve on 'stand-by'.

The *Bristol Queen*, (Capt. Jack George), for the first time in her career began the season, on Wednesday 17 April. She was due to be accompanied by the *Glen Gower* but a strike of shipyard workers at Bristol delayed her entry into service. The *Cardiff Queen*, (Capt. G. Gunn), was hastily prepared and brought out in her place for the Easter weekend; she maintained the ferry while the *Bristol Queen* took the down channel sailings.

On her first trip to Ilfracombe, on Good Friday 19 April, the *Bristol Queen* rescued three men in a dinghy in trouble off Sully Island. On Easter Monday she ran an unusually early trip to Lundy from Cardiff and Ilfracombe, and on the Sunday took the 'Easter Showboat' from Bristol and Cardiff to Ilfracombe.

This season saw a reduction in music and entertainment, the experiences of the previous two years indicating that it was fine weather rather than entertainment which attracted the majority of the public. This somewhat costly feature was not financially viable in the prevailing economic climate and was gradually reduced to two or three 'Showboats' per year.

The two *Queens* remained in service until Wednesday 1 May, when the *Bristol Queen* was chartered to take a party of German visitors from Swansea to Lundy Island; after her ferry trips on the following day she returned to Penarth Dock. The *Cardiff Queen* also finished at about the same time for completion of her winter overhaul.

The company's former managing director, Mr William James Banks, died in a Bristol nursing home at the age of eighty on Sunday 21 April. He had joined P&A Campbell Ltd. in 1897 after completing his engineering apprenticeship and established a small fitting shop in the Underfall Yard, at the seaward end of the Bristol City Docks, to enable the company to carry out its own repairs to its own steamers. Gradually, the works were extended and became an essential part of the company's business. In 1912 Mr Banks and Capt. Peter Campbell patented a design of piston rings and valves. Five years later the patent rights were purchased by the company and a subsidiary business, known as Campbell & Banks, was created. Mr Banks became a director in 1925 and, after the death of Capt. Alec in 1928, became joint managing director with Capt. Peter. He held that office for seven years until Peter retired, when he became sole managing director until his retirement in 1947.

The *Glen Gower* eventually began her ferry sailings on Saturday 4 May, under the command of Capt. Leo Virgo. On Wednesday 15 May, a day of deteriorating weather, potentially serious engine trouble was averted by her Chief Engineer, Alec Campbell. She had made two ferry crossings that

The Bristol Queen *on Penarth Pontoon. Sunday 27 January 1957.* (Norman Bird)

morning and had anchored off Weston during the low water period. The log book states:

> *At approximately 5pm, while proceeding from anchorage towards the pier in a gale force southerly wind, heavy confused sea and fierce rain squall, the master was informed by engineer Alec Campbell of an imminent breakdown to the main engine. Vessel was turned away from the pier and anchored while engineers investigated engine trouble. This was found to be a loose bolt, (later confirmed fractured), in the starboard eccentric straps. Under these circumstances it was not considered prudent to take the vessel to the pier, so vessel proceeded at 5.15pm, at reduced speed, to Cardiff. Remainder of sailings cancelled.*

She arrived at Cardiff at 19.00 and the trouble was rectified in time for her to resume her scheduled sailings on the following day.

Wild weather conditions were responsible for her being damaged on the evening of Saturday 24 August when, berthing at Weston in a heavy, following sea, she was thrown against the pier causing damage to her stem, fortunately above the waterline. Later that night the gale force winds delayed her again at Weston Pier, consequently she missed the tide on her return trip to Cardiff and had to spend the night at Barry.

The *Bristol Queen* re-entered service on Thursday 30 May. The *Cardiff Queen* followed on Friday 7 June and opened the Swansea season on the following day, Whit-Saturday. Both steamers experienced some minor boiler trouble early in the season but the recurring troubles encountered by the *Cardiff Queen* in the previous few seasons had been successfully remedied by the strengthening of the boiler supports.

For the first time for many years the company issued season tickets for the summer of 1957. At a cost of £7 7s 0d they offered unlimited travel in the Bristol Channel except for charter

The Glen Gower *leaving Ilfracombe on the afternoon of Thursday 13 June 1957; one of only three trips which she made down channel during that season. A prominent feature on her bridge is the radar apparatus, inherited from the* Empress Queen, *which was installed prior to the 1956 season.* (Lionel Vaughan Collection)

trips, sailings on Saturdays, Bank Holidays and throughout August Bank Holiday week.

With only three steamers in operation a reduction in services was inevitable. Trips out of Bristol were reduced by about half but on many of the 'No Sailing' days, combined bus/steamer trips were scheduled, passengers being conveyed to and from Weston to connect with the steamers there; an arrangement which was to continue for many years.

Sailings from Newport were abandoned entirely, the pontoon, owned by the Harbour Commissioners, having been sold to a Dutch company and towed to Holland for scrap. This meant that the annual charter trip by the Newport Harbour Commissioners, which usually took the form of a day trip direct to Ilfracombe, was somewhat different that year. The trip, on Saturday 22 June, began and ended at the south quay, Alexandra Dock, and the *Bristol Queen* cruised between the mouth of the River Wye and Minehead with a stop at Weston for lunch.

The weather that season was little better than 1956, with gales even more frequent. On Wednesday 10 July the *Bristol Queen* sustained a badly damaged bow when she struck Ilfracombe pier. The damage occurred above the waterline and temporary repairs were satisfactory. Permanent rebuilding was necessary during the following winter.

On Saturday 27 July she was on her way from Bristol to Ilfracombe with about 700 passengers, many of whom were 'singles', making their way to North Devon on holiday. The weather was atrocious but after sheltering at Barry for $1\frac{1}{2}$ hours she battled her way down channel taking nearly five hours for the $2\frac{1}{4}$ hour trip. She was in trouble again on Wednesday 28 August when, berthing at Weston in very nasty conditions, she hit the pier with her bow and the rocks with her stern; once again, temporary repairs were effected overnight. Apart from these altercations she had a relatively trouble free season mechanically and retired for the winter on Monday 30 September.

On a more amusing note, the Revd Norman Bird states:

> *The chief officer of the* Bristol Queen *that year was a Scandinavian, Mr Hansen; a most friendly officer indeed. Unlike Capt. George, he did not spend too much time on the bridge but was much happier looking after the social side of running the ship and fraternised cheerfully with all the regular*

The Glen Gower *at Barry Pier. 1957.* (Lionel Vaughan Collection)

> *passengers – which kept him pretty busy! He was of a very philosophical nature: I remember one day, late in the season, after various accidents had been encountered and many gales had been struggled through, the* Bristol Queen *arrived safely at Ilfracombe, well to time. As the gangways were put ashore Mr Hansen remarked to us,* 'Another triumph of navigation!'. *A catch phrase which has been handed down amongst Bristol Channel regulars to this day.*

The *Cardiff Queen* had also experienced a reasonably trouble free season. She finished her Swansea sailings and took over the ferry for a couple of days, while the *Glen Gower* was undergoing boiler repairs, until finishing her season on Saturday 21 September.

The south coast sailings had not been abandoned entirely, as originally planned. A limited service was maintained by the *Crested Eagle,* a twin screw diesel vessel of 245 gross tons, which was chartered from the General Steam Navigation Co. With a white funnel, incorporating the company's house flag painted on either side and under the command of Capt. J.W. Harris, (former master of the *Glen Gower*) she began her season on Sunday 2 June. On Thursday 6 June Capt. Harris left the company and was replaced by Capt. Neville Cottman, former chief officer of the *Bristol Queen.*

The *Crested Eagle* ran cruises between Brighton, Eastbourne and Hastings with trips to Shanklin, Isle of Wight, on Fridays: unfortunately she suffered a very bad season. During June and July she lost the equivalent of just over a week's sailings because of persistent engine trouble and about the same period owing to bad weather. The mechanical problems were eventually rectified but during August and September she lost no less than twenty-one days sailings because of bad weather.

The General Steam Navigation Co's motorvessel Crested Eagle, *on charter to P&A Campbell Ltd., arriving at Brighton. Friday 5 July 1957.* (Norman Bird)

The Cardiff Queen *stormbound at Ilfracombe at 08.15 on Sunday 25 August 1957. A newspaper report stated: 'A gale which swept across North Devon during the weekend damaged crops and property and left 350 Welsh visitors stranded at Ilfracombe on Saturday evening when their return sailing to Swansea had to be cancelled. They went home, instead, by the 20.42 train, and arrived home at 03.30 on Sunday morning. Steamer sailings remained cancelled on Sunday, when holidaymakers watched sheets of spray, often fifty feet high, break over the pier.' During the night she had almost broken away from the pier, recalling the similar occasion in 1950 when she had to run up channel for shelter. On this occasion, however, her moorings were increased and avoided mishap.* (Stanley Miller)

Later in the day she was moved from the Stone Bench further along the pier. In anticipation of the afternoon's 30ft high tide causing difficulties, her moorings were further increased to eight ropes, two wire hawsers, one of which was secured to the stone jetty at the entrance to the inner harbour, and a drag anchor dropped from her port sponson. Two large wooden fenders protected her starboard sponson from damage by ranging at the pier. In the event, the gale had abated somewhat by this time and she resumed her sailings on the following day unscathed. (Stanley Miller)

The Bristol Queen *arriving at Ilfracombe on Friday 30 August 1957, showing the temporary repair to her bow which had been damaged at Weston Pier two days before.* (Stanley Miller).

Her season ended on Monday 30 September when she left Newhaven to return to London. She was then advertised for sale by the GSN Co. and was purchased by Maltese buyers later in the year. This disastrous season marked the end of Campbell's regular association with the Sussex Coast.

The *Glen Gower* had also experienced a very bad season and on more than one occasion was nearly replaced by the 'stand by' *Glen Usk*. She was confined to the ferry and made only three trips down channel. Poor firing and her worn out boiler, with its continually fracturing tubes, meant that she ran very slowly and on several occasions she was so far behind schedule that she was unable to complete the full number of her advertised crossings, some having to be taken by the *Bristol Queen* after she had returned from her down channel sailings. Her final visit to Ilfracombe was made on the evening of Saturday 28 September, when she took the return journey of a day trip from Ilfracombe to Cardiff. She sailed from Cardiff at 19.25 via Penarth; took 1½ hours to cross from Barry to Minehead and arrived at Ilfracombe at 00.53 on Sunday 29, about two hours late. For most of the trip the boiler pressure was a mere 80 psi, only a half of what it should have been. She managed to complete her sailings and closed the season on Monday 14 October, entering Penarth dock on the following morning, never to sail under her own steam again. She was advertised for sale and by the end of the year one offer, of £6,500, had been received but was not accepted.

Soon after the season had ended the grim reality of the company's position became apparent. The cancellation of sailings on the South Coast resulted in an estimated loss of £7,000. The General Steam Navigation Co. reduced the charter fee for the *Crested Eagle* by £2,000 owing to the engine trouble experienced at the beginning of the season; the original charter fee is unknown. A bus strike in Swansea and the consequent difficulties for passengers travelling to and from the south dock entrance, caused an estimated loss of £5,000, and the additional cost of operating the two *Queens* at Easter cost an extra £1,500. The total trading loss for the season amounted to £35,953. Additional expenses were – £9,338 on the quinquennial surveys of the *Bristol Queen, Cardiff Queen* and *Glen Gower* and £4,374 on maintenance and repairs to the *Glen*

The bow of the Bristol Queen *undergoing permanent repairs in Penarth Dock in January 1958.* (Norman Bird)

Usk bringing the total debit balance to slightly under £117,400. The bank agreed to maintain an overdraft but how long the company could continue was a question on many people's minds!

After four consecutive Easters of fine weather, with two steamers in operation, the company tempted fate by bringing out three for the Easter of 1958. The *Glen Usk* (Capt. Virgo) re-entered service, in place of the *Glen Gower* on the ferry; the *Bristol Queen* (Capt. George) ran from Bristol and Cardiff to Ilfracombe, and the *Cardiff Queen* (Capt. Gunn) ran the first ever Easter trips from Swansea. The experiment, however, was not a success. Although the weather was dry, cold easterly and north-easterly winds persisted which kept the passengers away. After the holiday weekend the two *Queens* re-entered Penarth Dock to lay up until Whitsun.

The *Glen Usk*, after her year out of service, experienced a somewhat 'shaky' start to her season. Her departure from Penarth Dock for compass adjusting was delayed for a day because of engine trouble but she entered service on Maundy Thursday 3 April as scheduled. On Saturday 5 April, while berthing at Weston in the evening, the gale force NE wind and strong ebb tide set her down heavily on the face of the pier, causing damage to the starboard spring beam and star centre. Her sailings were not affected but the *Bristol Queen* replaced her for a few days after the holiday weekend to allow her to enter Penarth dock for repairs. She was back in service on Saturday 12 April having had the star centre repaired and a number of engine defects remedied: the spring beam was repaired later in the month.

In July 1958 the sixth British and Commonwealth Games were held in Cardiff. In anticipation of the week long event attracting a large number of visitors to the city, the company had advised the Games Committee of the sailings scheduled for the week and of certain fare concessions which were to be made available to team members and officials.

The Glen Usk *leaving the Pier Head, Cardiff, on Whit-Monday 25 May 1958.* (Jim Hendry)

The Bristol Queen *at anchor off Clovelly, Tuesday 26 May 1958.* (Norman Bird)

The Games were opened by HRH the Duke of Edinburgh on the evening of Friday 18 July before a gathering of 40,000 spectators and 1,500 competitors. HM The Queen was indisposed and unable to attend for the final four days as planned. However, the Royal Yacht, *Britannia* entered the Queen Alexandra Dock, Cardiff, as scheduled on the morning of Wednesday 23 July. The *Glen Usk* was in attendance off Penarth, giving her full complement of passengers a 'Grandstand' view of her arrival. The Games were a great success and indeed attracted many visitors but the number who availed themselves of sailing on the Bristol Channel appeared to be minimal. After the closing ceremony on the evening of Saturday 26 July, the Royal Yacht sailed, with Prince Phillip and Prince Charles aboard, for the Isles of Scilly. The *Glen Usk* dressed overall and packed to capacity, once again escorted her off Penarth.

The season continued with much bad weather. The *Bristol Queen* suffered paddle damage, owing to heavy seas, necessitating repairs being carried out in Cardiff on Friday 1 July. Her scheduled down channel sailing from Bristol on that day, instead of being cancelled, was taken by the *Glen Usk*. This visit to Ilfracombe was of some importance, incorporating a 'Special Publicity Cruise' from the North Devon resort, complete with entertainment from 'Thelma Hammond and her Ladies Orchestra' A somewhat embarrassing situation was created when, owing to a combination of heavy weather and her failure to keep up with the *Bristol Queen's* tighter schedule, the *Glen Usk* arrived at Ilfracombe one and a half hours late and the cruise had to be cancelled.

A newspaper cartoon referring to the summer of 1958.

The deteriorating weather at the end of July culminated in an appalling Bank Holiday weekend, the newspapers proclaiming it 'the worst since 1950' and even 'one of the worst in living memory'. Conditions were at their most deplorable on the Bank Holiday Monday, when a most unusual phenomenon occurred. A waterspout was sighted, sweeping up the channel. The 700ft high spiral churned up the water in its wake before it disappeared after about twenty minutes. Among its witnesses was the Porthcawl Harbour Master, Capt. Douglas Ide, who stated, 'I have never, in my seagoing experience, seen anything like this except at the start of a typhoon in the Caribbean'.

Earlier in the season the Chairman and Managing Director met with the Financial Controller, Mr William Walker, for further discussions regarding the company's future but the options put forward for consideration were overtaken by events which brought matters to a head.

Traditionally, the period between mid-July and mid-August was the busiest time of the season, when passenger figures were expected to reach their peak, but in 1958 the situation was reversed. What had been feared for some time came to pass.

The minutes of the board meeting of Tuesday 12 August 1958 included the following statement:

> *The Chairman and Managing Director met on Friday 8 August and, in consideration of the implications of the disastrous high season weather, agreed that unless fine weather prevailed until the end of the season, the company's position must be worse at the end of the year. The best interests of all would be served by the appointment of a Receiver for Debenture holders as soon as possible and, to this end, the necessary papers were drafted for despatch to Mr Walker.*

The board, with regret, unanimously agreed with this course of action. A further meeting took place on Wednesday 20 August at which the Chairman confirmed the appointment of Mr Walker as Receiver and Manager with effect from Friday 15 August 1958. The Board also agreed to recommend to Mr Walker that the stationing of a steamer at Swansea should be discontinued after the end of the 1958 season; that the Swansea office should be closed and the services of its full time agent should be dispensed with.

The Managing Director was asked to prepare for the Receiver's consideration a profile of the estimated income and expenditure likely to be incurred in running only two steamers in 1959. Mr Smith-Cox submitted the estimates and also wrote to the relevant local authorities on both sides of the channel, outlining the company's position and requesting a reduction in dues and charges if only two vessels were to use their landing facilities in the following year.

An atmosphere of gloom and despondency pervaded the ships and their personnel during the latter part of the season, exacerbated by the continuing poor weather.

The *Glen Usk* was experiencing a particularly grim season. On the night of Wednesday 27 August she was running about an hour late and at 23.00, while approaching the Pier Head, Cardiff, with the berthing signal at green, she slithered on to the mud about fifty yards short of the pontoon and remained there over the low water period. She refloated, undamaged, at 03.30 on the following day and was warped into her berth to discharge her 200 weary passengers.

On the afternoon of Wednesday 10 September, while approaching Weston in a strong ENE wind and tide down on the face of the pier, her steering gear jammed. She failed to lift off and rammed the pier with some force, causing considerable damage to her starboard sponson as well as the pier.

She was, as usual, due to close the season in early October but on the afternoon of Sunday 21 September she developed feed pipe trouble and entered Penarth dock on the following day to lay up for the winter. The *Cardiff Queen*, which had closed the Swansea season on Tuesday 16 September and had been running from Cardiff in place of the *Bristol Queen*, then took over the *Glen Usk's* sailings until the end of the season on Monday 6 October.

The *Bristol Queen* had entered Penarth Dock prematurely on Thursday 18 September. Enquiries for her charter, with a view to purchase, had been received from two sources; J. Gibson Johnson Ltd, for service in the Firth of Forth, and Messrs Kristensen & Drew Ltd, for running between southern Sweden and Denmark. Her early withdrawal from service was made with these possible charters in mind; neither, however, materialised.

At the board meeting on Wednesday 1 October two important matters were resolved. Proposals for the rebuilding of Minehead pier had last been discussed in August 1954 but had been shelved because of the company's financial position. Subsequently it had been decided that a replacement for the former pier was out of the question and that compensation for its wartime demolition should be sought from the Government. Protracted negotiations had continued until the autumn of 1958 when the claim was finalised and payment of £19,788 15s 3d was awarded, which the Receiver was pleased to accept.

Further good news followed when it was reported that in the light of the estimates submitted by Mr Smith-Cox, the Receiver was willing to run two steamers in the Bristol Channel during the 1959 season.

At the Annual General Meeting in Bristol on Friday 14 November, the Chairman, in a somewhat tantalising conclusion to his report, informed shareholders that 'conversations' were taking place between interested parties, with regard to the future of the company. He ended by saying:-

> *I am very hopeful that these conversations will be fruitful but it would be premature if I attempted to outline the directions in which they are leading.*

Furthermore, permission had been sought from, and granted by the Board of Trade for a deferment of the preparation of the company's accounts.

Despite the relatively optimistic tone of the meeting, an element of mystery, as well as uncertainty, now surrounded the company's future.

Early in 1959 Mr Smith-Cox informed the board that in reply to his requests of the previous August, the following reductions in landing charges had been negotiated for the forthcoming season:

South Wales Docks.	From £6,500	to	£3,250
Bristol	From £450	to	£150
Clevedon	From £150	to	Nil
Minehead	From £185	to	£5
Ilfracombe	From £750	to	£250
Bideford	From £25	to	Nil
Tenby	From £100	to	£25
Lynmouth Boatmen	Fifty per cent of previous charges.		

These reductions represented a saving of over fifty per cent – a good start to the year.

It was also announced that an enquiry had been received from Townsend Ferries regarding the possible charter of the *Bristol Queen*. When or where she would be employed was not mentioned but speculation arose with regard to No Passport trips from Dover to Calais. No further reference was made to the 'conversations' alluded to by the Chairman at the last Annual General Meeting but rumours began to circulate concerning a possible association between Townsend Ferries and P&A Campbell Ltd.

As the start of the 1959 season approached it became apparent that the two steamers in service would be the *Cardiff Queen* and the *Glen Usk*. The *Bristol Queen* was to remain laid up in Penarth Dock and would receive a minimal amount of maintenance.

The *Glen Usk*, with Capt. Neville Cottman in command, began sailing on Maundy Thursday 26 March and spent most of the season on the ferry. The *Cardiff Queen* (Capt. George) followed on Friday 14 May and maintained all other routes. The closure of the permanent station at Swansea inevitably meant a reduction in sailings from that port, but otherwise she was 'shared out' to give services as extensive as possible for one steamer.

For the first time since 1955 the company enjoyed a good season. Long spells of fine weather, aided by the innovation of local television advertising, led to encouraging passenger figures. Less than a week's sailings in total were cancelled because of bad weather – an exceptional summer by recent standards. The *Glen Usk* missed half a day's sailings on Good Friday because of furnace repairs and the *Cardiff Queen* spent two separate days in August undergoing paddle repairs in Barry Dock but mechanical problems were the exception rather than the rule.

Only a few incidents marred the otherwise successful season. One was of such a potentially serious nature that it made front page news in all the local newspapers. It involved the *Glen Usk* and to appreciate the situation fully, some background information may be necessary.

The journey up and down the River Avon is fraught with hazards; the tidal flow, bends and mudbanks calling for precise navigation and specific timing. The most dangerous part of the river is the Horseshoe Bend, a sharp, semi-circular curve bordered by fields on the Somerset side and an 80ft cliff on the Gloucestershire side. On fast flowing spring tides a safe passage can be accomplished only within 1½ hours either side of high water. Before or after that period, apart from the obvious problem of insufficient water over low tide, the river flows at such a rate that a ship inward bound on the flood or outward bound on the ebb, would run a grave risk of being swept on to the mud at the Horseshoe Bend. On the slower neap tides the timing is a little less critical but the hazards remain.

The *Glen Usk*'s schedule for Sunday 30 August 1959 was to leave Cardiff at 12.40 for Penarth, Weston, Clevedon and Bristol, with a cruise to Walton Bay, then departing from Bristol at 18.15 for Clevedon, Weston, Penarth and Cardiff. High water at Bristol was at 17.14.

On her return to Bristol from the Walton Bay cruise she was delayed on the journey up river by a large number of inward bound ships. Consequently she left Hotwells landing stage, on the return journey to Cardiff, half an hour late, and approached the Horseshoe Bend at 19.10, nearly two hours after high water. While negotiating the bend, the ebb tide forced her wide of her course and pushed her starboard side on to the mud of the Gloucestershire bank, where she gently shuddered to a halt. Her engines were put astern and ahead in an attempt to free her but she quickly settled into the mud and ran a serious risk of damaging her starboard paddle.

The Glen Usk *aground on the Horseshoe Bend in the River Avon on the evening of Sunday 30 August 1959.* (Chris Collard Collection)

In the early hours of Monday 31 August 1959, the Glen Usk *lies high and dry on the river bank, illuminated by the Fire Brigade's floodlights. The gangway which had become wedged between the bank and the starboard sponson had to be cut away with axes.* (Chris Collard Collection)

Immediately, one of the seamen tied a heaving line around his waist, jumped from the port side and attempted to swim to the opposite bank but the current was too strong for him and he was hauled back on board by his colleagues. Several of the crew then launched the stern lifeboat and rowed across the river with lines from both bow and stern. They succeeded in putting the ropes ashore but she defied all attempts to haul her off.

At 19.30 Capt. Cottman instructed all 600 passengers to disembark by way of two gangways from the starboard sponson. By this time the Police and Fire Brigade had arrived on the scene and they assisted the passengers off the gangways, along 100 yards of muddy river bank, up a 50ft steel ladder, across a railway line and up a further rough track to the Portway, the main road from Avonmouth to Bristol. From there alternative transport had been arranged to take them to their destinations. The safe removal of all the passengers was a commendable feat and had been accomplished by 20.00, just as the daylight was beginning to fade. It was conducted in an orderly and organised manner and, although the elderly and infirm found the climb a considerable ordeal, only three people were reported to have needed minor medical attention.

At 20.30 all the crew were ordered ashore. The ship's papers and log books were removed and the Purser, Mr J. Keating, took charge of the strong-box containing the day's takings.

Low water was at 23.34 and as the tide receded she was left high and dry, inclined at an angle of 40-45 degrees. The portholes and sponson doors on the port side were secured; coal was heard falling against the side of the port bunker; barrels tumbled in the bar and furniture toppled. The fires had been damped down and the stokehold doors were closed. Under stress from the changing tide the ship lurched and creaked to the accompaniment of the continuous, gentle hiss of steam from her safety valve. By midnight the last of the spectators, who had gathered on the Portway, made their way home.

A somewhat lighter episode in the night's proceedings is recounted by Nigel Coombes in his book, *Passenger Steamers of the Bristol Channel:*

> *There was nothing more to be done before the officers and crew settled down to their lonely, night long vigil. One final visitor, however, turned out to be the most welcome of them all in the person of Mr Dawson, the resourceful manager of the Grand Spa Hotel. Having heard of the* Glen Usk*'s unexpected predicament, and weighing up the effects of a chill, autumnal night on the health of a dispirited ship's crew, Mr Dawson judged the situation perfectly. Immaculately attired in black coat and striped trousers he stepped through the muddy detritus of the foreshore, with full professional aplomb, bearing his ship's provisions. In such an unlikely venue for a delivery, was a case of Navy Rum ever received more unexpectedly or consumed more gratefully?*

In the early hours of the morning the Fire Brigade, who had illuminated the ship with floodlights, placed buoyancy tanks under the port sponson to assist her re-floating. They also cut away a gangway which had been left on the after starboard sponson and which, as the ship heeled over, slipped and firmly wedged itself between the bank and the underside of the sponson.

High water was at 05.54 on Monday 31 August. At 03.00 she began to right herself, the officers and crew re-boarded her and she was afloat by 03.45. At 04.00 two tugs arrived and made fast, the *Bristolian* forward and the *John King* aft. The emergency dynamo was started,

The tugs John King, *(left), and* Bristolian *towing the* Glen Usk *from the South Pier, Avonmouth, on the morning following her grounding in the River Avon.* (Chris Collard Collection).

navigation lights lit and, with two red 'Not Under Command' lights at her foremast, the tugs began towing her down the river. She arrived at Avonmouth at 06.10 and berthed at the South Pier, where a preliminary inspection indicated that no water was entering the hull and that she was fit to be towed to Penarth. She left Avonmouth at 09.10 and dropped her port anchor in Penarth Roads at 12.37, to await the tide. At 17.00 she entered Penarth dock and was put straight on to the pontoon. On the following day she was inspected and minor repairs were carried out to her starboard paddle but, otherwise the staunch old ship was found to be little the worse for her experience. She resumed her normal sailings on Wednesday 2 September, but the episode was not quite over.

The port anchor, dropped when she arrived in Penarth Roads on Monday 31 August, could not be winched back on board as the vessel was out of steam. Accordingly, a buoy was attached to its chain and dropped over the side, its bearings being noted, for retrieval at a later date. Meanwhile, a substitute anchor was borrowed from the laid up *Glen Gower*. A few weeks later an attempt was made to recover the original; a search was made for the marker buoy but it was never found! It is possible therefore that the *Glen Usk's* anchor lies in the mud, off the Penarth sea front, to this day.

Tragedy occurred aboard the *Cardiff Queen*, at Ilfracombe, on the morning of Sunday 13 September when her Chief Engineer, Alec Campbell collapsed and died while working in the engine room shortly before the ship was due to sail. Mr Campbell, aged sixty-two, was the younger son of Capt. Peter and the last surviving member of the Campbell family associated with the company.

A steering fault led to a very short day trip for the *Cardiff Queen's* passengers on Tuesday 22 September. She left Cardiff for Minehead, Lynmouth, Ilfracombe and Lundy at 09.00. The trouble occurred as she approached Penarth and she anchored off the Outer Wrack Buoy, the *Glen Usk* passing her shortly after, on her first crossing of the day to Weston. The problem was traced to her telemotor steering gear, but despite extensive work by the engineers, the fault could not be rectified. On her return from Weston at 11.25, the *Glen Usk* moored alongside, took off her passengers and returned them to Cardiff. Half an hour later the *Cardiff Queen* proceeded to the Pier Head using her emergency hand steering gear.

This entailed fitting the large steering wheel, normally lashed to her stern rail, to the rudder post on the after deck, thus by-passing the telemotor. Owing to the weight of the rudder, two helmsmen were necessary. Their line of sight forward being totally obscured, the steering instructions were relayed verbally from the master on the bridge, via a 'chain' of seamen, to the mate at the stern who confirmed the orders for the helmsmen.

The *Cardiff Queen* was back in service on the following day and continued her sailings until retiring to Penarth dock for the winter on Monday 28 September. She was joined by the *Glen Usk* a week later on Monday 5 October. The fine summer resulted in a net trading profit of £15,100.

The mystery of the 'conversations' referred to by the Chairman at the Annual General Meeting of 1958 was solved when, on 8 December 1959, the shareholders were informed by letter of the proposals for the company's future. Iain Hope, in his book *The Campbells of Kilmun*, concisely sums up the situation:

> *Sydney Smith-Cox approached Roland Wickenden, a fellow accountant, for help. A keen weekend yachtsman and businessman, Roland Wickenden was at that time running George Nott Industries Ltd, whose main activities were house building and the operation of Townsend Ferries, their recently acquired, but long established one ship, car ferry company. The appeal from Mr Smith-Cox struck a responsive chord, which was perhaps surprising. He had little to offer a potential investor, P&A Campbell Ltd was a near bankrupt company with ageing ships, falling traffic and a pile of debt. By contrast Roland Wickenden headed a small but rapidly growing, profitable business group and had high ambitions for the future. Among other things he wanted to expand the Townsend car ferry operations but heavy taxation of company profits made this difficult. Smith-Cox and Wickenden, with their accountancy training, realised that through one of the oddities of British tax law, Campbells' accumulated trading losses could be offset against the profits of Townsends to reduce the latter's tax bills. This freed money to allow Townsends to increase its investment in new car ferries. So a deal was struck whereby, on 31 December 1959 George Nott took over all the assets and liabilities of P&A Campbell Ltd. It gave Wickenden and his company a small but useful boost in the early days of their cross channel operations. For Smith-Cox and his team, it was to give P&A Campbell Ltd a remarkable 'Indian Summer'.*

1960/1964 – All Change, No Change

The declining number of paddle steamers around the coast of Great Britain instigated, in 1959, the formation of the Paddle Steamer Preservation Society; a body of enthusiasts dedicated, not only to preservation, but also to the promotion of paddle steamer travel. Their efforts to stimulate in the general public an awareness and interest in this dying form of transport were sorely needed as paddle steamer operators faced the continuing challenges of alternative leisure pursuits.

For the White Funnel Fleet, however, the new decade began with the future looking more assured than for many years. The Annual General Meeting, held in Bristol on Monday 29 February 1960, dealt with the business of the sixteen months from 1 January 1958 to 30 April 1959, to bring the accounting period into line with that of George Nott Industries. The directors' report stated:

> *The re-organisation of the company...is now complete. While of necessity the weather must continue to play a very large part in the company's results, your directors hope that a more prosperous period is now being embarked upon.*

Paradoxically, the most striking effect of the take-over was the apparent lack of change. The company still traded as P&A Campbell Ltd and the management remained the same, although Roland Wickenden joined the board in February 1960.

As for the steamers, developments had taken place concerning the *Glen Gower*. Enquiries had been made with regard to her charter for excursions in the Brighton area, but it appears that a faster steamer was needed. Offers of £4,800 and £5,100 had been received for her purchase, both of which had been refused. She was finally sold to the Belgian shipbreakers Van den Bossch, and left Penarth dock, in tow of the Hull-based tug *Tradesman* on the afternoon of Thursday 7 April 1960.

Her engine had turned over for the last time, on her entry into Penarth Dock, on Tuesday 15 October 1957; on that date it was the oldest operational paddle steamer engine in the country! When the White Funnel steamer *Albion*, (Ex *Slieve Donard*), of 1893, was broken up at Troon after the First World War, her engine was dismantled and kept in storage for installation in the new steamer then under construction at the Ailsa Shipbuilding Co.'s yard. That steamer was launched in February 1922 as the *Glen Gower* and was destined to become one of the company's most versatile and hard worked steamers, both in the Bristol Channel and on the south coast.

A small group of people witnessed her departure on that spring afternoon. Her hull and funnels were badly rusted and her foremast had been removed; shipped into the *Cardiff Queen* after her own had been found to be partially rotten. Her final journey took her to the River Scheldt and ended on Tuesday 12 April, when she arrived at the breakers' yard at Boom, near Antwerp.

The 1960 season began on Maundy Thursday 14 April with the *Glen Usk* (Capt. Virgo), followed on Saturday 28 May by the *Cardiff Queen* (Capt. George). The pattern of sailings

The United Towing Company's tug, Tradesman, *alongside the* Glen Gower *in Penarth Dock, Sunday 3 April 1960.* (John Brown)

The Tradesman *and the Cardiff tug,* Boxmoor, *(astern), tow the* Glen Gower *into Penarth basin. Her foremast and two of her lifeboats had been transhipped into the* Cardiff Queen. (Norman Bird)

After several days' delay owing to gales in the English Channel, the Glen Gower *finally departs on her last journey on Thursday 7 April 1960. She arrived at the breakers yard at Boom, Antwerp, on Tuesday 12 April. Despite rumours that she had been sold to Smits, the Dutch towage company, for use as a storeship, she was broken up soon afterwards.* (Norman Bird)

was virtually identical to that of the previous year. The River Avon continued to 'cast its spell', causing the *Cardiff Queen* to touch the mud on the Gloucestershire bank of the Horseshoe Bend while making her way to Bristol late on the night of Saturday 30 July. Two paddle arms were slightly damaged but her sailings were not affected. She left Hotwells on the following morning bound for Clevedon, Barry, Mumbles and the Gower Coast and while rounding the Horseshoe Bend, with the wind and flood tide on her port bow, took a sudden sheer to the Gloucestershire bank. She was immediately stopped to prevent her grounding and although Capt. George used the engines and helm to bring her bow back to midstream, she would not lift off sufficiently. By coincidence, the tug *John King* had followed her down river bound for Avonmouth, and, in passing, her crew took the *Cardiff Queen's* bow rope and assisted her to clear the bank and resume her journey.

At the beginning of August 1960 the Welsh National Eisteddfod was held in Cardiff. The Royal Yacht *Britannia*, with the Duke of Edinburgh aboard, sailed overnight from Cowes to dock at Cardiff on the morning of Friday 5 August. The Queen and their children arrived by train and the whole family attended several of the Eisteddfod events before leaving in the *Britannia* for Orkney and Shetland on the evening of Saturday 6 August. The arrival and departure of the Royal Yacht were accompanied by the usual flotilla of flag-bedecked escorts, including the *Glen Usk*.

The season drew to its close with the *Cardiff Queen* retiring on Monday 26 September, followed by the *Glen Usk* on Tuesday 11 October, both vessels having run well with very few mechanical problems. The weather was a different matter, and unlike 1959, reverted to its former unsettled state, causing a number of cancellations.

The board meeting on Tuesday 27 September began with Mr Smith-Cox's report of the 1960 season. He summed up by stating:

> *In spite of the appalling summer weather, if the cost of repairs during the winter were no more than the previous year, the company would end up on the right side when the accounts are prepared in April next.*

The trading profit for 1960 turned out to be £28,950.

Several options were then put forward for consideration with regard to the future of the *Bristol Queen*. An enquiry for her purchase had been received from the USA, and the Dutch agents acting for the American company were to be instructed that the ship was available at a cost of £75,000.

A somewhat startling announcement was then made by Mr J. Bowles, Secretary of Nott Industries, concerning an expansion of the company's services. He reported on investigations he had made in the south of France regarding the operation of a vessel based at Nice. It was agreed that Mr Smith-Cox should visit the area to inspect the landing facilities of the resorts in the vicinity and to discuss, with the relevant harbour authorities, the viability of such a project.

Mr Smith-Cox then informed the meeting that the Board of Trade had intimated that there might be a further relaxation of the regulations governing no-passport trips to the Continent, including the abolition of photographs on identity cards which, he said, 'much mitigated against business'. It was agreed that if such modifications were implemented, preparations would then be made to send the *Bristol Queen* to the south coast as an experiment 'on our old station'.

Mechanically the *Bristol Queen* was ready to sail; she had been taken on to the Penarth pontoon in July 1960 when steam had been raised and her engines turned over slowly. The options put forward for her future were likely to be the subjects of protracted negotiations, therefore, it was also decided that if no alternative employment could be found for her, she should operate in the Bristol Channel during the following season. The *Cardiff Queen* would be prepared as a relief ship and that in future seasons the two vessels should alternate on a similar basis as consorts to the *Glen Usk*.

By the end of January 1961 plans had changed for a variety of reasons. Nothing more had been heard from the American company regarding the purchase of the *Bristol Queen* and no further news was forthcoming concerning the modification of the no-passport regulations. Mr Smith-Cox had visited the south of France and reported on his findings with regard to the landing facilities in the vicinity of Nice. The ports inspected were suitable for steamer operations except for two harbours, where construction work would be necessary, and several other resorts where small boats would have to be used to embark and disembark passengers. The whole project, however, appears to have been approached in a very half hearted manner; no further developments ensued and the undertaking came to nothing.

Early in 1961 the *Glen Usk's* five-yearly board of Trade survey revealed that she was in a very sound condition; no hull plates needed replacing but repairs were necessary to her keel, estimated at a cost of £2,000. Consideration was being given to her conversion from coal to oil firing and until this matter was resolved the repairs would be held in abeyance. Therefore she was to remain laid up and the *Queens* would be brought into service. The *Bristol Queen* would start at Easter and run at weekends only until May; her crew, during the intervening weeks, being utilised to complete the overhaul of the *Cardiff Queen* in time for her to begin sailing at Whitsun.

After two years of inactivity the *Bristol Queen*, with Capt. George back on the bridge of

The Cardiff Queen, Bristol Queen *and* Glen Usk *in Penarth Dock on Sunday 12 March 1961. The* Queens *are being prepared for the forthcoming season, but the* Glen Usk *was destined to sail no more under her own steam.* (Chris Collard)

his former command, left Penarth dock for compass adjusting on Wednesday 29 March 1961 and began the season, from Cardiff on the following day.

In mid-April she was chartered by BP Ltd for a cruise from Pembroke Dock. While in West-Wales the opportunity was taken to run a day trip from Milford Haven, via Tenby, to Ilfracombe which took place on Tuesday 18 April. On the following afternoon she made her way to Pembroke Dock in readiness for her charter trip on Thursday 20 April. It was a particularly short cruise of only one hour's duration which took her passengers to view the new BP oil terminal in Angle Bay. After disembarking the charter party at Pembroke Dock she sailed at 18.15 to return direct to Cardiff. This was the only visit of a White Funnel paddle steamer to Pembroke Dock in the post-war years and the first day trip from Milford Haven to Ilfracombe in over thirty years.

The *Cardiff Queen* entered service on Friday 19 May with Capt. Virgo in command. Both steamers then alternated between the ferry and down-channel sailings throughout the season.

In order to make the running of these two costly units of the fleet financially viable, the network of sailings became extended. The ships and their personnel were required to work extremely long, arduous hours.

With virtually no time available for maintenance, mechanical problems became more and more prevalent and placed an additional burden on the already overtaxed engineers.

For several years the author has enjoyed a frequent and prolific correspondence with the former P&A Campbell engineer, Mr Roy Barclay, now living in retirement with his wife, Phyll, in South Devon. Mr Barclay's phenomenal memory has given rise to a number of fascinating accounts of incidents from his White Funnel days.

In the years shortly before the Second World War he was apprenticed to Charles Hill & Son of Bristol. After serving in tankers on the Russian convoys during the conflict he returned to Hill's as a marine fitter in 1946 and was instrumental in the installation of the engines of the *Bristol Queen*. He joined P&A Campbell Ltd in the mid-1950s and served aboard the *Glen Usk*, *Cardiff Queen* and *Bristol Queen*. Although each vessel brings her own

The Cardiff Queen *at the Pier Head, Cardiff, on Saturday 20 May 1961. A seaman on the after deck hands a rope to the boatman who will secure it to a bollard on the quay wall. On her departure this rope will be used to swing the ship around, and point her seaward.* (Chris Collard)

particular memories for him it was the *Bristol Queen* in which he served longest and which he holds in the highest esteem. He lamented her two year lay up and states:

> *In 1961 we were having a load of paddle trouble, especially with the radius rods and their nuts, bolts and pins. we were using parts that should have been scrapped many years before and actually had to wind hemp from old rope around the threads to make the nuts fit tightly.*

The expertise and stamina of the engineering department was fully put to the test on Wednesday 9 August 1961 when the *Bristol Queen's* day trip from Cardiff to Ilfracombe and Lundy turned out to be a very long affair. Mr Barclay takes up the story:

> *At Lundy, after the last passengers had returned to the ship and the anchor was up, our engine room telegraph went to slow ahead. I was second engineer working the 'Golden Levers'. Our usual chief, Reg Nieth, was on leave and Charlie Morgan was acting in his place. Our third was David Rich – he was new to paddle steamers but was most willing to learn.*
>
> *Our telegraph had gone to 'Full Ahead' and just as we cleared Lundy a loud banging was heard coming from the paddle box. Immediately, I stopped* Bristol Queen's *mighty steam engine. I told David to open the watertight paddle door in the engine room alleyway very carefully as he was all dressed up in his uniform. The wind was getting up and a nasty sea was running. As soon as he released the last clip the door swung inboard with a great gush of sea-water; he was soaked!*
>
> *I put the high pressure piston at the end of its stroke, shut the throttle lever so that the engine would not turn over and put the sign* 'DO NOT MOVE ENGINE' *on the controls. I then went out on to the paddle to investigate the source of the trouble.*

A radius rod pin had worked loose and had fallen out. The rod itself had become bent and had to be removed completely. Roy Barclay was the only engineer with experience of this type of work and took charge of the situation.

> *I asked the mate to let us have some of the deck crew to help us. After the rod had been removed we secured the float as best we could with wire ropes and bottle screws. All this took about two hours, after which we set off again very slowly. Capt. George rang down on the bridge phone and asked if we could give him a little more speed. I gave the throttle lever a few more notches but straight away the banging started again. We stopped the engine and had to go out on to the paddle once again to secure the float.*

This proceedure was repeated no less than eight times, the last being carried out just as the ship was approaching Ilfracombe at 21.50 and necessitating her anchoring about 100 yards off the pier.

> *We had secured the float again and were waiting for the telegraph to ring to go alongside the pier, but – nothing. I went to the bridge and asked Capt. George what was happening. He told me that the deck crew could not get the anchor up – it was somehow caught under the keel. After a while they managed it and we went alongside at midnight. The 1½ hour trip from Lundy to Ilfracombe had taken nearly eight hours! It was only then that I had my tea! The chief told me to go and rest but I couldn't – I was too worried.*

Above and previous page: The Bristol Queen *at Porthcawl on the afternoon of Sunday 25 June 1961.* (Chris Collard)

Meanwhile, in response to a radio message sent from the ship earlier that evening, the Ilfracombe Harbour Master had arranged for a supply of chains and large bottle screws to be delivered to the pier. These were used to replace the temporary lashings, the work taking over two hours.

The log book for Thursday 10 August states:

> *02.30 Float secured by chains and bottle screws.*
> *02.35 Left Ilfracombe.*
> *02.50 Rillage Point abeam.*
> *04.05 Foreland Point abeam.*
> *05.00 Stopped to tighten screws and lashings.*
> *05.12 Proceeded.*
> *05.24 Nash Point abeam.*
> *06.15 Breaksea lightvessel abeam.*
> *06.52 Sully Island abeam.*
> *07.38 Berthed at Pier Head, Cardiff.*

Permanent repairs were carried out during the day and she was back in service on Friday 11 August.

Towards the end of the season the *Cardiff Queen* suffered a recurrence of the steering trouble which had afflicted her during the previous year, and on three separate occasions she had to be

The Bristol Queen *arriving at the south lock entrance to Newport Docks on the return of the 'Inspection of the Port' charter trip by the Newport Harbour Commissioners on Friday 30 June 1961. This was an event which had taken place annually, except for the war years, on the last Friday in June since the 1890s.* (Chris Collard)

brought home on emergency hand steering gear. After the third breakdown, on Thursday 3 October, she was withdrawn from service owing to the unreliability of her steering telemotor. To avoid cancellations the *Bristol Queen*, which had retired for the winter on Tuesday 19 September, was brought back into service until the end of the season on Monday 9 October.

Despite the poor weather the steamers were reasonably well patronised throughout the season and produced a net trading profit of £26,585.

Owing to the closure of Penarth dock alternative winter quarters had been secured at the eastern end of the Roath dock, Cardiff. The *Glen Usk* had been towed there during October. Her future appeared to be very much in the balance and dependent on the proposed changes to the no-passport regulations which were still under discussion by the Board of Trade. In the event of a favourable outcome the *Bristol Queen* would be stationed on the south coast and the *Glen Usk*, hopefully converted to oil firing, would resume sailing in the Bristol Channel in company with the *Cardiff Queen*. In the meantime, however, plans were made for the following season for the two *Queens*.

They entered the Bute Dry Dock, Cardiff, together in mid-March 1962 for about ten days. The *Cardiff Queen* (Capt. Virgo) opened the season on Thursday 19 April, followed by the *Bristol Queen* (Capt. George) on Thursday 31 May.

For the first time since the pre-war years a day trip from Cardiff, via Ilfracombe, to Milford Haven took place on Sunday 24 June 1962. The day was fine and sunny but a strong NW wind on top of a heavy swell produced a nasty sea, even in the upper reaches of the channel. The *Bristol Queen* was late arriving at Ilfracombe and there were fears that the crossing to Milford would have to be cancelled or that a trip to Lundy might be substituted. However, she left Ilfracombe at 12.40, forty minutes late, and set off across the channel with the wind and sea on her port bow. It was a rough crossing and her speed had to be reduced to 'slow ahead' at one stage but she demonstrated her sea-going qualities to great effect and arrived at Milford Haven, only one hour late, at 16.45. A one-hour cruise in the Haven had been advertised which took place despite her late arrival and attracted a large number of local residents. This 'Trip of the Season', as it was billed in the timetables, became an annual event until 1966, always taken by the *Bristol Queen*

The otherwise uneventful season was yet again one of poor weather with cancellations all too frequent. The *Cardiff Queen* retired for the winter on Tuesday 25 September, leaving the *Bristol Queen* in service until Monday 1 October. This was the earliest ending to a season since the war and, more significantly, the last to be made by a paddle steamer!

In an attempt to alleviate the persistent mechanical problems experienced by the *Bristol Queen* during the previous two seasons it was considered advisable for her to receive some specialist attention. One of the last outposts of paddle steamer operations south of the Clyde was Weymouth, where the ships of the Cosens fleet underwent their winter maintenance. It was arranged for the *Bristol Queen* to be placed in their hands for a thorough overhaul.

She sailed from Barry on Monday 12 November at 11.50 and arrived off Weymouth just after 08.00 on the following morning, having covered the 272 mile journey at an average speed of 13.5 knots. She was piloted into the harbour by Capt. Holyoak, one of Cosens masters, and moored at the Custom House Quay. Next day she passed through the road bridge to the inner harbour and was berthed at Cosens yard in preparation for the work to begin.

The Chairman's report of the 1962 season was brief. He stated that a newly formed associated company within the George Nott organisation had taken over the majority share

The Bristol Queen *and* Cardiff Queen *in the Bute Dry Dock, Cardiff, on Saturday 24 March 1962.* (Chris Collard)

The Bristol Queen *arriving at Weymouth on Wednesday 14 November 1962.* (John Brown Collection)

holding in Birnbeck pier, Weston, at a cost of £26,000 and it was anticipated that 'in due course this should be of benefit'. The newly opened Butlins Holiday Camp at Minehead had provided a useful, if not spectacular source of Saturday revenue. Through bookings were available from Cardiff and Barry to Weston, then by coach to Minehead, and vice versa.

The season produced a net profit of a mere £6,220. It was increasingly apparent that the operation of two large paddle steamers was becoming something of a financial burden. They were big ships to fill, and although during the high season they paid their way, the early and late season running, often with a very small complement of passengers, cut deeply into the company's profits.

In looking at the overall coastal passenger scene the company's attention was drawn to the plight of the Liverpool & North Wales Steamship Co. Ltd, which had gone into voluntary liquidation on 19 November 1962. At that date the long established company owned two contrasting, screw driven vessels – the *St Tudno*, of 2,326 gross tons, and the *St Trillo*, of 314 gross tons. It was the latter vessel which attracted the interest of the directors of P&A Campbell Ltd. With her passenger capacity of about 600 and her economy of operation she was considered to be a viable proposition for running in place of the *Queens* in the Bristol Channel in the early and late season.

In February 1963 a number of North Wales interests made offers for her but she was eventually purchased by Townsend Ferries for operation by P&A Campbell Ltd. The purchase price was not disclosed but it was in excess of the highest other offer of £17,500 and included the goodwill of the North Wales coast trade.

The *St Trillo* had been built by the Fairfield Shipbuilding & Engineering Co. Ltd at Glasgow as the *St Silio*. On her trials on 15 April 1936 she reached a speed of 13.75 knots but her two, six-cylinder diesel engines, by Crossley of Manchester, were designed to give a service speed of 12 knots. On release from Admiralty service in November 1945 she took the name of a former paddle steamer of the Liverpool company – *St Trillo*.

The Liverpool & North Wales Steamship Co.'s motorvessel St Trillo, *at the Pier Head, Cardiff, on arrival from Menai Bridge. Wednesday 13 March 1963.* (Chris Collard)

The St Trillo, *now painted in Campbells' colours, moored astern of the* Glen Usk *in the Bute East Dock, Cardiff, on Sunday 7 April 1963.* (Chris Collard)

Her first journey to the Bristol Channel began after dry-docking at Birkenhead when she left the Mersey on the morning of Saturday 9 March 1963, arriving at Menai Bridge that evening. There she was delayed by heavy weather until the following Tuesday and finally reached the Pier Head, Cardiff, on the morning of Wednesday 13 March. A trial run to Weston pier, at which she acquitted herself well despite a strong southerly wind, took place on the following day before she entered the East Bute dock, Cardiff, for painting in Campbells' colours.

Under the command of her former master, Capt. Owen Williams, she opened the 1963 season, on the ferry, on Maundy Thursday 11 April, with visits to Bristol on Saturday 13 April and Ilfracombe on Tuesday 16 April. The *Cardiff Queen* accompanied her during the Easter weekend, taking most of the longer sailings, before re-entering dock for the completion of her winter overhaul.

The purchase of the *St Trillo* made the future of the *Glen Usk* even more uncertain. In addition, the Government restrictions on cross channel trips had not been sufficiently relaxed to encourage the company to resume continental sailings. The *Bristol Queen* would not, therefore, be sent to the south coast but would be available for Bristol Channel work; this made the *Glen Usk* even more surplus to requirements. The anticipated cost of her conversion to oil firing was £30,000. Furthermore, her condition had deteriorated over the previous two years and the total cost of bringing her back into service, including oil firing, would have been a prohibitive £45,000.

She was advertised for sale and within a matter of weeks was sold to Haulbowline Industries. She left Cardiff for the breakers' yard at Passage West, Cork, on the evening of Monday 29 April 1963, in tow of the Alexandra Towing Co.'s Swansea-based tug *Talbot*.

The *Glen Usk* was the last of the company's pre-First World War paddle steamers. Built by the Alisa Shipbuilding Co. of Troon and launched in 1914 she, like the *Britannia*, was the third of a trio of almost identical steamers. Her predecessors, the *Lady Ismay* of 1911 and the *Glen Avon* of 1912, were fine ships but the *Glen Usk* was a 'masterpiece', incorporating many of the ideas and innovations suggested by Campbells' senior master of the time, Capt. Dan Taylor. Regarded by many of the company's personnel as the finest sea-boat of the fleet, she was a familiar visitor to all the Bristol Channel ports but never ran on the south coast, apart from a brief visit for the Coronation Naval Review in 1937. Since 1946 she had become something of an institution on the Cardiff to Weston ferry and had endeared herself to many thousands of holidaymakers on both sides of the channel.

The *Bristol Queen* left Weymouth after her winter overhaul on Saturday 27 April 1963 and arrived at Cardiff on the following day. She entered service on Saturday 11 May with Capt. George in command, shortly before running the first weekend excursion to Penzance and the Isles of Scilly since before the First World War. Such trips were not uncommon in the 1890s and 1900s and were operated by a number of Bristol Channel companies. The last is believed to have been that of the *Britannia* in July 1907, when the return fare was £1 0s 0d; in 1963 the fare was £9 0s 0d. The trip began on Friday 17 May from Cardiff and Weston. She then left Ilfracombe at 14.00 with 120 passengers for a calm and uneventful voyage to Penzance, picking up her pilot in Mount's Bay at 21.10. She was issued with a special Class 2 Board of Trade certificate for the trip allowing her to carry 144 passengers and forty-one crew, making a total of 185 – the capacity of her six lifeboats.

She berthed at the Albert pier overnight and left for the Isles of Scilly on the following morning. After boarding her pilot off St Mary's she took the high water route through Crow Sound into the harbour at Hughtown to berth astern of the Isles of Scilly Steamship Co.'s regular ferry, *Scillonian*. After disembarking her passengers she anchored in the roads between St Mary's and Tresco until

The Glen Usk *being manoeuvred into the Roath Basin in preparation for her departure for the breaker's yard, Monday 29 April 1963.* (Chris Collard)

The Glen Usk *leaving Cardiff for Passage West, Cork, on the night of Monday 29 April 1963.* (Chris Collard)

The Bristol Queen *leaving Penzance for the Isles of Scilly on Saturday 18 May 1963.* (John Brown Collection)

The Bristol Queen *at Hughtown, St Mary's, Isles of Scilly. Saturday 18 May 1963. She is returning to the jetty after lying at anchor offshore.* (John Brown Collection)

after the departure of the *Scillonian* at 16.15. The *Bristol Queen* sailed two hours later, this time taking the low water route through St Mary's Sound, to the south of the island. After another night at Penzance, during which she was moored alongside the *Scillonian* at the Lighthouse pier, she returned to Cardiff. The trip was highly successful and was to be repeated in subsequent years.

Under the command of Capt. Phillip Power, former Chief Officer of the *Bristol Queen*, the *Cardiff Queen* entered service on Saturday 25 May, allowing the *St Trillo* to return to North Wales in time to commence her season from Llandudno at Whitsun.

A milestone in Bristol Channel history was reached in July 1963 with the introduction of a hovercraft service between Penarth and Weston. In the autumn of 1961 the company made an application to the Air Transport Licensing Board for permission to operate hovercraft. Negotiations followed which came to fruition when the company, in association with Westland Aircraft Ltd, introduced the world's first cross-channel hovercraft service.

The 27 ton SRN-2 hovercraft arrived in Cardiff docks aboard the coaster *Bay Fisher* and began the service between the beaches of Penarth and Weston on Thursday 23 July 1963. Forty-two passengers could be carried; the crossing took just under fifteen minutes, and six crossings, totally free from tidal restrictions, were made daily. The single fare was £1 0s 0d; return tickets were issued at £1 7s 6d with the return journey being made by steamer. The service was well patronised, perhaps more because of its novelty value than anything else, and ended on Friday 30 August. The hovercraft left Cardiff, again aboard the *Bay Fisher* for Devonport, from where, over the following two weeks, it was engaged in Royal Naval exercises in the River Dart. The company stated, 'Much valuable experience was gained which will assist us in our long term plans to establish regular services with hovercraft crossing the Bristol Channel and elsewhere.'

The paddle steamers maintained the usual varied, but arduous, programme of sailings throughout the season. There were hardly any cancellations despite the poor weather and mechanical problems were few.

The Milford Haven pilot boarding the Bristol Queen. *Sunday 28 July 1963.* (Chris Collard)

The Bristol Queen *approaches the Milford dock entrance after her cruise in the Haven. Sunday 28 July 1963.* (Norman Bird)

Shortly after leaving Bristol on the morning of Saturday 10 August the *Cardiff Queen* was delayed for about an hour while her condensor was cleared of an influx of River Avon mud. Unfortunately some adverse publicity arose from the incident when the press erroneously reported that she had run aground.

The *Bristol Queen* finished her season on Thursday 19 September somewhat prematurely owing to paddle trouble, and the *Cardiff Queen* followed on Sunday 29 September. Both vessels were moored for the winter at the south end of the Queen Alexandra dock, Cardiff.

The *St Trillo* had enjoyed a satisfactory season in North Wales. She sailed regularly from Llandudno to Menai Bridge with cruises in the Menai Straits; an almost identical service to that provided in her previous ownership but now, without the 'competition' from her larger sister, the *St Tudno*, her passenger figures were higher and the service was more profitable. On Saturday 22 July she made the first call by an excursion vessel at Caernarvon since 1934 and also completed the first 'Round Anglesey' cruise since 1947 on Saturday 10 August. She sailed from Menai Bridge on Saturday 14 September, arrived off Penarth on the following day and commenced running on the ferry on Thursday 19 September, continuing until Monday 21 October, the latest closing of a season for many years.

On the following morning she left Cardiff for Port Dinorwic, near Caernarvon, where she was to spend the winter. At just after 04.00 on Wednesday 23 October, in high winds and fog, she struck a rock near Portdinllaen, Caernarvonshire, and was held fast by the head. Rescue services were alerted, including a helicopter from RAF Valley, Anglesey, and the Portdinllaen lifeboat. Non essential members of the crew were taken ashore but she refloated after four hours. Accompanied by the lifeboat and taking on water, although within the capacity of her pumps, she proceeded under her own power to Port Dinorwic, where she arrived at about 17.00. After temporary patching she spent most of November at the Birkenhead yard of Grayson, Rollo & Clover undergoing permanent repairs, before returning to Port Dinorwic for the rest of the winter.

The Chairman stated, in his annual report, that the deplorable weather had adversely affected the passenger steamer operations although a considerable increase in trade had taken place in connection with Butlin's Holiday Camp at Minehead. The net operating profit was £29,370. This, however, included the North Wales service and the profit from the Weston Pier Co. From 1963 onward these figures were combined and a breakdown of the individual elements is not recorded.

At the board meeting in September certain information was imparted by the managing director, which passed without comment, discussion, or elaboration but which, in retrospect, was highly significant. He stated that he had written to British Railways and Red Funnel Steamers Ltd regarding the possibility of purchasing one of their south coast, screw diesel vessels for service in the Bristol Channel. Both companies had replied that they had nothing available at the time but if and when such a situation arose, P&A Campbell Ltd would be advised.

After the momentous events of the previous season 1964 was a relatively quiet year with a good summer of long, sunny spells and many hot days. In contrast, however, the season opened with the coldest Easter since 1922. After several delays because of bad weather the *St Trillo* arrived in the Bristol Channel to begin the sailings on Maundy Thursday 26 March.

At the beginning of May the Swedish liner *Kungsholm*, (21,000 gross tons), brought her American passengers to the Bristol Channel as part of a European cruise. She anchored in Walton Bay early on the morning of Monday 4 May for a two day visit. The *St Trillo* was chartered to act as tender and landed her passengers at Avonmouth, where coaches were waiting to take them on tours of the local countryside, including visits to historic buildings and gardens.

The *Kungsholm* left Walton Bay on the evening of Thursday 5 May, bound for Llandudno, and followed by the *St Trillo*, which again acted as her tender in North Wales. In addition to her tendering duties the *St Trillo* returned north in order to fulfil a ten day charter for the Mersey Docks & Harbour Board at Liverpool, where she was engaged on a variety of cruises throughout the dock system for trade representatives.

Meanwhile the *Cardiff Queen* (Capt. Power) had entered service on Saturday 9 May, followed by the *Bristol Queen* (Capt. George) on Wednesday 13 May.

On Whit-Monday 18 May the *Bristol Queen* had the misfortune to fall heavily against Weston pier when she cracked her starboard spring beam, bent two radius rods and dented a float in her starboard paddle. Temporary repairs enabled her to make her last ferry crossing at half speed but she entered the Mountstuart Dry Dock on the following morning for four days, while permanent repairs were effected.

The *St Trillo* arrived back in the Bristol Channel on Sunday 24 May and took over the ferry for a week while the *Bristol Queen* made her second, annual weekend excursion to Penzance and the Isles of Scilly from Saturday 30 May to the following Monday. On her return the *St Trillo* once again went north to begin her season at Llandudno.

The *Cardiff Queen* ran into trouble on the afternoon of Sunday 14 June while bound from Weston to Clevedon, with forty-six passengers, for a return trip to Barry. As she approached Clevedon, on the ebb tide, it became apparent that she was running into very shallow water; the log book states:

15.14 *Reduced speed.*

15.16 *Vessel aground. Clevedon pier head bearing east by 3 miles. Engines worked ahead and astern but vessel held fast.*

15.19 *Starboard anchor dropped. Soundings taken around vessel. Bilges examined – vessel*

	not taking any water. Wind W by N, force 3 to 4.
16.25	*Sand dried out. Master, Mate and Chief Engineer went on sand and inspected position of hull. Found to be lying firmly supported on sand from stern to forward wing. Forward of that point vessel was suspended from six inches to two feet off the sand. Vessel steady and in upright position throughout grounding.*
17.15	*Tide turned.*
18.15	*Sand covered.*
19.01	*Vessel afloat and swinging at anchor.*
19.06	*Anchor aweigh. Engines astern. Proceeded.*

She then returned to Weston and resumed her ferry sailings none the worse for her experience.

The fine weather was interrupted in mid-September by a severe south-westerly gale. On Wednesday 16 September, mountainous seas kept the *Bristol Queen* stormbound at Swansea and gave the *Cardiff Queen* a particularly rough time on the ferry. She had great difficulty in berthing at Weston on her afternoon crossing and ranged so violently at the pier that her small number of passengers had to disembark, one by one across the wildly lurching gangway. She quickly cast off and very cautiously backed away from the pier, meeting the full force of the oncoming seas. On her arrival at Cardiff all further sailings for the day were cancelled.

The *St Trillo* had completed the North Wales season on Monday 14 September but the same gale delayed her return to the Bristol Channel. She was stormbound at Holyhead until Thursday 17 September and arrived at Cardiff next day.

The following weekend saw the revival, by the *St Trillo*, of two trips from years past. On Saturday 19 September she sailed from Barry to make the first call at Watchet since 1929. The local residents turned out in force to greet her and to avail themselves of the cruise calling at Minehead. On the morning of Sunday 20 September she took over 300 passengers on a day return trip from Chepstow to Clevedon, Weston and Barry. This was the first visit of an excursion vessel to Chepstow since 1914.

These two trips were accomplished just in time; on the following day it was discovered that she had developed a number of serious mechanical problems which needed immediate attention. The repairs, which included the fitting of new cylinder linings and piston heads were carried out at Barry and kept her out of service until Wednesday 30 September, her sailings, in the meantime, being shared between the two *Queens*.

The *Cardiff Queen* retired for the winter on Monday 28 September and the *Bristol Queen* two days later, leaving the *St. Trillo* to close the season on Monday 12 October, returning to Port Dinorwic on the following day.

The Chairman's report of the season stated:

> *...the weather, at the time that mattered, was very favourable. As a result there was a considerable increase in business, both in the Bristol Channel and North Wales. I am convinced that as travelling by road is now frequently so uncomfortable, given reasonable weather the indications are that there is likely to be a return to travelling for pleasure by sea.*

How ironic that one of the major factors which contributed to the company's decline in the 1950s should now be having the opposite effect!

The Cardiff Queen *was forced to make a hasty departure from Weston owing to dangerous conditions in a south-westerly gale on the afternoon of Wednesday 16 September 1964.* (Chris Collard)

1965/1966 Bad Summers and Breakdowns

1965 heralded the beginning of the final episode in the lives of the White Funnel paddle steamers. It was the company's worst season since the war. The light airs and calm seas, which predominated the previous summer, gave way to much more boisterous conditions which rivalled 1950 in terms of bad weather. Additional problems were caused by a high incidence of accidents and breakdowns. The company avoided excessive cancellations by a remarkable 'juggling act' which usually involved the steamers in performing extra sailings in addition to their already gruelling schedules.

The *St Trillo*, after a stormy passage from North Wales, began the season on Maundy Thursday 13 April. Her Master, Capt. Owen Williams, had now obtained a Bristol Channel license and therefore no longer needed the services of a pilot, Capt. Power having performed that duty during the previous two seasons. She experienced a foretaste of the disruption to come that summer during her short, early spell in the Bristol Channel. On the evening of Easter Saturday 17 April she had great difficulty in berthing at Weston pier in strong winds and had to make a rapid departure, leaving about twelve passengers behind who had to make the journey home to South Wales by train. Her Ilfracombe sailing, scheduled for the following day, was cancelled because of heavy weather and on Monday 26 April she crossed to Weston but was unable to berth at the pier because of heavy seas. She returned to Cardiff where the rest of the day's sailings were cancelled. However, she successfully accomplished her visits to Chepstow, on Saturday 1 May, and on the following day, to Watchet where 290 passengers braved the heavy rain for the trip to Minehead. After returning to Barry that evening she left straight away for North Wales.

The *Bristol Queen* (Capt. George) had entered service on Saturday 1 May and, on the following Tuesday and Wednesday, acted as tender to the *Kungsholm*, which again visited the Bristol Channel and anchored in Walton Bay. A similar service was provided by the *St Trillo* when the liner anchored off Llandudno on Thursday 6 May.

The *Cardiff Queen* (Capt. Power) began her sailings on Wednesday 19 May, allowing the *Bristol Queen* to make her annual Isles of Scilly excursion from Saturday 22 May to Monday 24. The trip was a success but she experienced a very rough passage to St Mary's which resulted in a late departure from Penzance, on the return to Cardiff next day, while welders repaired a damaged paddle.

During the post-war years, it was the writer's custom to keep a detailed account of the day to day activities of the steamers. In view of the ensuing, chaotic and complex nature of the season, the trials and tribulations which the company encountered are recounted by quoting from those diaries:

The St Trillo *leaving Ilfracombe on a cruise to Bideford Bay early in the 1965 season.* (Chris Collard)

The St Trillo *arriving at Cardiff in 1965.* (Chris Collard)

The Bristol Queen *passing Pill, in the River Avon, on Tuesday 11 May 1965. On the bridge, Capt. George raises his cap to wave to the occupants of the Pill ferry; an ancient crossing which connected the riverside villages of Pill and Shirehampton.* (Chris Collard)

Sunday 20 June.
The Bristol Queen *ran the 'Summer Showboat' from Bristol and Cardiff to Ilfracombe. On the return journey, paddle trouble developed as she arrived at Penarth Pier. Her Bristol passengers, including the performers, complete with their instruments, (except the piano!), disembarked and were transferred to the* Cardiff Queen *which took them to Weston, where coaches were provided to take them home. The* Bristol Queen *limped into Cardiff after anchoring off Penarth, where temporary repairs had been effected. The damage – a broken radius rod – was repaired overnight and she was back in service next day.*

Thursday 8 July and Friday 9 July
Cardiff Queen *out of service because of boiler trouble.*

Friday 16 July.
The Cardiff Queen *berthed at Weston in the early evening with a capacity crowd of passengers, most of whom were waiting to disembark, causing a considerable list to starboard. The ebb tide forced her against the pier where one of the piles made contact with the starboard bridge wing causing it to crumple like paper. She ran, for the next few days, with the wing roped off until repairs were carried out with plywood sheeting.*

In the hazy morning sunshine of Sunday 20 June 1965, the Bristol Queen *lies alongside Hotwells Landing Stage, Bristol, awaiting her departure on the 'Summer Showboat' trip to Ilfracombe, with music and entertainment aboard. The people seen on the landing stage are the performers and include the drummer, complete with two drums; the female singer, wearing the light coat and a scarf covering her 'beehive' hairstyle, so characteristic of the 1960s, and three burly gentlemen with the unenviable task of getting the piano aboard – always a difficult, yet fascinating feat, frequently 'assisted' by much advice from 'experts' who, from a safe distance, shouted instructions as to how best to do it. As far as the author is aware, no piano was ever lost overboard during the operation! (Chris Collard).*

The Bristol Queen *about to leave the Pier Head, Cardiff, on Whit Sunday 6 June 1965.* (Chris Collard)

Wednesday 29 July

A particularly wild day! Bright and sunny but with a gale blowing from the west. The Bristol Queen *sailed from Bristol, bound for Weston, Barry, Mumbles and the Gower Coast. I embarked at Weston and Capt. Wide, (who was relieving Jack George for a few days), took her to Barry between the Flat and Steep Holms – a very turbulent stretch of water at the best of times, but particularly so today. I went up to the reserve deck to watch the fun. As I reached the top of the companionway I saw a massive sea approaching and grabbed the rail just in time! The bow seemed to rise forever; she shuddered on top of this wall of water and then plunged headlong into a deep trough only to crash into another enormous roller which sent Capt. Wide and the mate, Ray Hardcastle, reeling from one side of the bridge to the other; the helmsman just about managed to stay on his feet. On arrival at Barry there was some doubt as to whether the trip would proceed. She carried on, however, and after passing Nash Point steamed into a 'boiling cauldron' of a sea in Swansea Bay. After a most uncomfortable passage she arrived at Mumbles an hour late and the Gower Coast cruise was cancelled. On her return across Swansea Bay she rolled very heavily and off Porthcawl was struck by a huge sea which broke against her starboard side. She heeled violently to port and a mass of heavy spray drenched the passengers on deck. Saloon furniture, crockery, glasses and bottles crashed below and the force of the sea stove in one of the portholes of the forward saloon. The thick, heavy glass landed a few feet inboard on the deck of the saloon, and water poured in. Fortunately, no one was near it at the time and the hole was quickly plugged. Later that evening the gale made it virtually impossible for her to berth at Weston. She eventually managed to make the pier and a number of passengers disembarked but the operation was so precarious in the violent conditions and so many ropes parted that it was considered prudent to beat a hasty retreat, even though many of the Weston passengers were still aboard. She made her way to Portishead where all the remaining passengers disembarked and were taken to their various destinations by coaches. The log book entry for the day ended by stating:*

> 'A total of six attempts were made to berth at Weston. Weather throughout the day – Westerly gale, Force 8/9. Heavy seas. Vessel rolling and pitching violently.'

Sunday 8 August.
The Bristol Queen *ran a very successful trip, promoted by the Paddle Steamer Preservation Society, from Swansea and Ilfracombe to Padstow. About 750 passengers were aboard for the first such sailing since the* Devonia *visited the Cornish port, thirty years before, on Sunday 7 August 1938.*

Monday 9 August.
The Bristol Queen *was due to bunker at Swansea last night, on her return from Padstow, but the road tanker failed to arrive. She had sufficient fuel to cross to Ilfracombe this morning and arrangements were made for her to take on oil there. Unfortunately, the fuel was delayed, with the result that her trip to Clovelly had to be cancelled and about 800 potential passengers had to be turned away on one of the finest days, so far, of this terrible summer.*

Sunday 16 August.
The Cardiff Queen *was backing out of Barry harbour at full speed, having sounded the statutory three blasts on her whistle, when she encountered the small coastal tanker* Wheeldale H, *'sneaking' around the west breakwater and entering the harbour against the signal. The tanker struck the* Cardiff Queen *on the port quarter, denting the saloon strake and pushing in three dining saloon portholes. Fortunately the saloon was empty, no passengers were hurt and there was no damage below the waterline. After an inspection by surveyors at Barry Pier she was allowed to complete her day's sailing with a tarpaulin sheet covering the damage and the after part of the dining saloon roped off. She spent the next three days in Cardiff Dock while the damaged plates were replaced.*

Tuesday 24 August.
During the night, heavy seas battered the Cardiff Queen *while sailing light up-channel from Swansea to Barry. Abdul the steward told me, 'All of the catering staff went to bed but it was impossible to sleep, I was thrown out of my bunk three times! We all got up, went into the after deck shelter – and held on!' The ship suffered paddle damage as a consequence of the weather, which necessitated repairs on the following day. The down channel trip was cancelled when the* Bristol Queen *was required to take over the ferry.*

Passengers embarking on the Bristol Queen *at Lynmouth in 1965. This operation was performed 'on the run', while the vessel steamed slowly ahead, and was normally accomplished without difficulty.* (Chris Collard)

One evening, however, a strong easterly wind developed shortly after the steamer had left Ilfracombe for the return journey to Cardiff. Off Lynmouth a very nasty sea was running, nevertheless, Campbell's agent and chief boatman, Tom Richards, a seaman of considerable experience, was confident that he could effect the transfer safely. He is seen here approaching the Cardiff Queen, *with his passengers huddled behind a tarpaulin, while he and his crew become extremely wet. The boat was brought alongside the leeward sponson of the steamer and the passengers were safely boarded.* (Chris Collard)

Wednesday 8 September.

A morning of heavy rain and winds which steadily increased to gale force. The Bristol Queen *had sailed from Cardiff to Ilfracombe but did not proceed to Bideford, as scheduled, and remained at the Stone Bench. The* Cardiff Queen *battled her way from Swansea to Ilfracombe and sailed for Lundy but the weather deteriorated and on approaching the island she turned back after a huge sea had, yet again, pushed inboard her forward, starboard rail. On her arrival off Ilfracombe she radioed to the* Bristol Queen *to clear the Stone Bench to allow her to berth, the heavy sea precluding her berthing at the face of the pier. There was a considerable delay in the* Bristol Queen *replying as most of her officers were taking advantage of their cancelled trip to snatch a few hours sleep. In the meantime the* Cardiff Queen *circled off Ilfracombe in the gale with her passengers and crew becoming more and more frustrated by the delay. Eventually the* Bristol Queen's *rather shamefaced company moved her along the pier to allow the* Cardiff Queen *to berth astern of her at the Stone Bench.*

On Thursday 9 September the *Cardiff Queen* was out of service at Barry with radius rod trouble. The *Bristol Queen* was also afflicted with paddle trouble while returning up channel from Ilfracombe that evening. Second engineer Roy Barclay has occasion to remember the incident vividly:

Between Minehead and Barry a radius rod pin came out of the starboard star centre. We stopped the engines and with a very rough sea running we went out into the paddle box. I stood on the star centre while the chief, Reg Nieth, stood on the boss of the wheel with a spare pin to hand to me. Suddenly the ship rolled heavily to starboard and the paddle box became almost full of water. After it had drained away I looked across and was relieved to see Reg still standing there. The water was freezing; however, we managed to replace the 4" diameter pin and were soon back in the engine room – soaked to the skin!

The major event of 1965 was the purchase of the twin screw, diesel vessel *Vecta*, (630 gross tons), from the Southampton, Isle of Wight & South of England Royal Mail Steam Packet Co. Ltd. Built by J.I. Thornycroft & Co. of Southampton and launched in 1938, she ferried passengers and up to twelve cars between Southampton and the Isle of Wight, her last crossing having been made on Saturday 18 September 1965. She was officially handed over to P&A Campbell Ltd, at Southampton, on the morning of Monday 20 September and sailed at 14.00 for Cardiff, via Ilfracombe and Swansea. She commenced sailing on the ferry on Friday 24 September, retaining her Red Funnel Fleet colours until the end of the season.

On the same day the *Bristol Queen*, on her return from Ilfracombe to Barry and Cardiff, left Minehead harbour on a very high tide. She damaged her starboard paddle when it scraped against the harbour wall as the sponson mounted a guard beam, and had to return to Cardiff at half speed. On the following morning the *Cardiff Queen*, which had retired to the Queen Alexandra Dock on Wednesday 22 September, was brought back into service to replace her.

At the end of her season, the *Bristol Queen*'s master, Capt. Jack George, retired. He had joined the company in the 1900s, worked his way through the ranks to become Campbell's senior master and took command of the *Britannia* from the late 1920s until the outbreak of the war in 1939. During the hostilities he held command of the turbine steamer *Empress Queen*, remaining with her for her first civilian season. He took over the *Bristol Queen* in 1948 and remained with her for

The Bristol Queen *at Padstow, Sunday 8 August 1965. The return trip, from Swansea and Ilfracombe, was promoted by the Paddle Steamer Preservation Society and was the first call at the Cornish port since the* Devonia's *visit thirty years before.* (Chris Collard)

each of her post-war seasons until his retirement. He was a quiet but courteous man whose knowledge and experience of the Bristol Channel were vast. To mark the end of his career he was presented with a specially commissioned oil painting by the marine artist, John Nicholson, of the *Bristol Queen*, by the South Wales Branch of the World Ship Society.

On the evening of Friday 24 September the *Cardiff Queen*, making her way up the River Avon, ran on to the Horseshoe Bend on an ebb tide. After a few minutes she scraped herself off, damaging her port paddle wheel in the process, and dragging on to her deck several branches from the overhanging trees which had become entangled in the paddle box lamp standards. Welders spent most of the night repairing the paddle damage to enable her to resume her sailings on the following day.

She finally retired for the winter on Monday 4 October in an extremely dilapidated condition. As she left the Pier Head for the Queen Alexandra Dock an onlooker remarked that she looked more like a vessel which had seen service on the Russian convoys rather than in the Bristol Channel!

Capt. Jack George, for many years Commodore of the White Funnel Fleet, who retired at the end of the 1965 season. (Edwin Keen)

The Master of the Cardiff Queen, *Capt. Phillip Power, in 1965. Following Capt. George's retirement, Capt. Power took command of the* Bristol Queen *from 1966.* (Chris Collard)

A Chapter of Accidents

The Cardiff Queen *at Ilfracombe pier, showing the repair to her bridge wing after being damaged at Weston pier on Friday 16 July 1965. On the port side of the bridge sit Captain Leo Virgo and his wife. Captain Virgo joined the company in the early 1950s and held command of most of the White Funnel steamers, including the* Cardiff Queen, *until leaving the company at the end of the 1962 season.* (Chris Collard)

The Cardiff Queen *in the Queen Alexandra Dock, Cardiff, on Tuesday 17 August awaiting repairs to her port quarter, which was damaged in a collision with a tanker off Barry on the previous day.* (Chris Collard Collection)

The damaged plates have been removed and replacements are about to be welded in place. (Chris Collard)

The Cardiff Queen *at Barry on Wednesday 25 August 1965, showing the temporary repair to her stern, complete with 'painted' portholes. Actual portholes were cut during the following winter.* (Chris Collard)

The broken teak rail and bent stanchions of the starboard bow, forced inboard by heavy seas in Swansea Bay on the night of Tuesday 24 August 1965. (Chris Collard)

The Cardiff Queen *leaving the Pier Head, Cardiff, to enter Cardiff dock at the end of her 1965 season, Wednesday 22 September 1965.* (Chris Collard)

The *Vecta* made a number of trial trips, including a call at Bristol and a charter trip for the Port of Bristol Authority to off Sharpness and back to Avonmouth. She closed the season on Monday 11 October and sailed from Cardiff on the following day, for Weymouth, where she was to receive a thorough engine overhaul at Cosens Yard.

Her arrival in the Bristol Channel coincided with the best spell of weather that summer and she attracted a large number of passengers. She performed well but 'paddle steamer diehards' complained of her restricted deck space, noisy engines and smell of diesel oil. However, her economy of operation would, it was hoped, subsidise and extend the lives of the *Queens* which, with their soaring running costs, were becoming a considerable financial headache. The Chairman's report of the season stated:

> *1965 was an all time record for appalling summers. Each month recorded the most rainfall, the coldest weather and the least sun. In consequence the number of passengers diminished.*

Plans for the 1966 season were awaited with some apprehension; how would the arrival of the *Vecta* affect the paddle steamers? The minutes of the board meeting at the end of January 1966 state:

> *In deciding whether or not three vessels should be in service in the Bristol Channel in 1966, after an examination of figures it was agreed that if revenue from fares increased by £30,000 it would prove profitable. It was decided that, as an experiment, this should be done. This would enable us to augment our services considerably, but whether these increased facilities will continue must, of course, be dependent on the results of our experience in 1966.*

The new year began ominously when the *Vecta* made two attempts to return from Weymouth but had to turn back on each occasion because of engine trouble. Her third attempt was successful and she arrived in Cardiff on the morning of Saturday 19 February and berthed in the East Bute Dock.

P&A Campbell's newly acquired motorvessel, Vecta, *at the Pier Head, Cardiff. Wednesday 22 September 1965.* (Chris Collard)

She entered the Mountstuart Dry Dock on Monday 28 February as the *Vecta*, and emerged on Monday 21 March as the *Westward Ho*. The small, car-carrying area on the forward main deck was plated in and converted into a saloon; six small windows being cut into the plating on both sides. Following the Campbell tradition, a cowl was fitted to her funnel and she was painted in her new colours in readiness to begin the ferry sailings on Maundy Thursday 7 April 1966, with Capt. Ray Hardcastle in command.

The vagaries of the British weather reached an extreme on Thursday 14 April, when all of her sailings were cancelled because of heavy snow! Otherwise she ran well until the end of the month when she spent a few days in dock while, on the instructions of the Board of Trade, an additional bulkhead was built into the new forward saloon.

On Tuesday and Wednesday 3 and 4 May she tendered the Swedish liner *Gripsholm*, (sister ship of the *Kungsholm*), which anchored in Walton Bay as part of the annual 'Spring Adventure' cruise.

The *Bristol Queen* (Capt. Power) left Cardiff Dock for compass adjusting on Wednesday 18 May. A few hours later, while lying at the Pier Head, a leak was discovered in her boiler. Its repair necessitated the cancellation of the forthcoming week's sailings and included the postponement of the annual Isles of Scilly excursion. After re-entering service on Wednesday 25 May she was dogged by intermittent steering trouble but was able to carry out the rescheduled Isles of Scilly weekend from Saturday 11 to Monday 13 June. On her return, however, she was taken out of service for two days for further maintenance.

The *Cardiff Queen* had been rushed into service earlier than planned, in less than immaculate condition, to enable the *Bristol Queen* to run the Isles of Scilly weekend, then docked again, on Friday 17 June for the day, during which her overhaul was completed. She was

The renamed Westward Ho *in the Mountstuart Dry Dock, Cardiff, on Saturday 12 March 1966.* (Chris Collard)

commanded, for that season only, by Capt. E.J. (Jack) Wide, a former Campbell master who, since the war, had been Pier Master at Weston's Birnbeck Pier.

Some disruption to sailings from Cardiff occurred on Friday 24 June when one of the sixty-year-old pontoons at the Pier Head sank, only a short while after the *Westward Ho* had embarked her passengers for Weston. Divers found an 18in hole in the pontoon which was repaired by the following Sunday. In the meantime, the Cardiff sailings were re-routed via Penarth or Barry.

The pattern of sailings in 1966, with three ships in operation, hardly changed but, as promised by the Chairman, there were more trips all round. The *Queens* took most of the down channel sailings while the *Westward Ho* maintained the ferry and up channel services. Calls at Chepstow were not resumed but the latter made her first calls at Watchet and Minehead on Saturday 18 June.

On Thursday 23 June a leak in one of her bottom plates caused the cancellation of the *Cardiff Queen*'s morning sailing from Swansea. A Board of Trade surveyor supervised the fitting of a cement box over the damage which enabled her to complete an evening charter cruise towards Tenby, although the cruise was curtailed, at the request of passengers, because of rough weather. She made her way up channel that night and on the following morning entered dry dock at Cardiff for permanent repairs to her bottom plates.

While taking the down channel sailing from Cardiff on Sunday 26 June she was instructed to delay her departure from Penarth Pier in order to embark a 'party' who had missed her at Cardiff and who were to be trans-shipped from the *Westward Ho*. The motorvessel berthed alongside the *Cardiff Queen* shortly after and the 'party' – consisting of one person – embarked in grand style amid the cheers and applause of the passengers

The *Queens* had received routine maintenance only during the winter and mechanical problems soon began to occur on an alarming scale. In spite of persistent paddle and steering defects, the *Bristol Queen* managed to cope with the majority of her sailings. Many of them took place in appalling weather, including the annual Milford Haven trip on Sunday 10 July, when she encountered heavy rain and a force eight gale. The cruise from Milford was cancelled and she was further delayed on the return journey owing to bad visibility.

She made the first of three scheduled calls at Padstow on 28 July. Her trip began from Swansea and Mumbles and a connection was provided from Barry, via Ilfracombe, by the *Westward Ho*.

On Saturday 30 July the *Cardiff Queen* experienced paddle trouble, for the third time that month, near the Copperas Rock, off Combe Martin, when a driving arm fractured, causing her and her 150 Swansea passengers to be stranded at Ilfracombe overnight. Her limping progress to the pier was accompanied by the lifeboat and a helicopter, which were exercising in the area, and attracted some unfortunate and inaccurate publicity. She was towed back to Cardiff from Ilfracombe on the following day by the Swansea tug *Cambrian* and resumed sailings after repairs on Thursday 4 August.

Thick fog shrouded the whole of the South Wales coast on the morning of Friday 19 August. The *Cardiff Queen*, bound for Ilfracombe, proceeded no further than Mumbles Pier, having taken 1½ hours to reach there from Swansea. The *Bristol Queen* left Cardiff, with visibility down to about fifteen yards at times, and attempted to berth at Penarth pier. She missed the jetty completely and her waiting passengers described how she suddenly loomed out of the fog and bore down on the pier at a point about three quarters of the way along its length from the landward end. She backed away and disappeared into the fog to make a second attempt but again approached the same spot. This time her bow made contact and the ebb tide quickly swung her around, bringing her starboard side on to the pier. Her 120 passengers then disem-

Dwarfed by the huge Channel Dry Dock, the Cardiff Queen *receives attention to a leak in one of her bottom plates on Friday 24 June 1966.* (Chris Collard)

barked and the *Westward Ho,* which arrived safely at the jetty, making full use of her recently installed radar, took many of them on her trip to Minehead. At that stage the damage to both the *Bristol Queen* and the pier was relatively minor. A Cardiff tug then arrived to tow her off but in doing so the ebb tide caused her to bump several times causing further damage to the pier. The *Bristol Queen,* needing only minor attention, anchored off Barry and returned to Cardiff that evening in order to resume sailing on the following day. The pier damage was repaired during the course of the following few months and although extensive, costing in the region of £8,000, the repairs caused no disruption to the sailings.

The *Cardiff Queen* had a slightly less harassing season than the *Bristol Queen* but both steamers experienced a considerable amount of boiler, paddle and steering trouble over the following few weeks. Gales also predominated the latter part of August and caused a number of cancellations.

Since 1964 regular cruises up the River Severn had enabled passengers to follow the progress of the building of the Severn Road Bridge. Having reached its completion it was opened by HM The Queen on the afternoon of Thursday 8 September. The *Bristol Queen,* dressed overall and carrying 1,000 passengers, turned just short of the bridge as the motorcade crossed over it after the opening ceremony. Although an occasion for celebration, the day was nevertheless tinged with sadness as it marked the last day of operation of the old Beachley to Aust car ferry, the final crossing taking place a few hours after the bridge was opened. The *Bristol Queen* returned to Cardiff with considerable clanking and banging emanating from her engines and paddles and it was with some relief that she retired to the Queen Alexandra dock on the following day.

The *Cardiff Queen* struggled through the next couple of weeks and took the third of the

The Bristol Queen *alongside Penarth pier in a somewhat unusual position on the foggy morning of Friday 19 August 1966.* (Chris Collard Collection)

The Westward Ho *arriving at Ilfracombe in August 1966.* (Chris Collard)

An advantage of the Westward Ho *was her manoeuvrability in confined waterways. Here she has entered the outer harbour at Ilfracombe and is using her twin propellers to swing around to berth at the Stone Bench 'bow out', in readiness for a quick departure. August 1966.* (Chris Collard)

season's trips to Padstow, on charter to the Paddle Steamer Preservation Society, on Sunday 11 September. She was late leaving Swansea because of paddle trouble and had to cancel the scheduled cruise in the River Camel. This was her only visit to the Cornish port. On her last day in service, Wednesday 21 September, she ran a well patronised trip to Lundy which, although no one realised at the time, was to be her final passenger sailing. She entered the Queen Alexandra dock on the following day.

The *Westward Ho* rounded off the season on Monday 17 October and left for Cosens yard, Weymouth, on the following Wednesday. She had to shelter overnight in the lee of Lundy owing to heavy weather and arrived in Weymouth on Friday 21 October. After an engine overhaul she arrived back at Cardiff on Thursday 22 December.

The seasons of 1965 and 1966 stand above all others in the history of the White Funnel Fleet. At no other time had the company faced such a series of calamities on so great a scale!

The Chairman's report stated:

> *The summer of 1966, if one can call it such, has now passed. Amongst other problems with which we had to contend was the effect of the seamen's strike. I am happy to say that no strike took place so far as our company's vessels were concerned and I would pay tribute to the way in which the National Union of Seamen honoured their agreements with us. Nevertheless, prospective passengers, reading about strikes and expecting that one would probably take place, were loath to make party bookings, or indeed to come to the boats to travel at all, and we missed a lot of business as a result. Disasters to small motor launches around the country had quite illogical and most deplorable effects upon our business, since although our vessels are scrupulously maintained and certified by the Board of Trade, many prospective passengers decided not to travel by sea.*

The atmosphere of uncertainty surrounding the future of the paddle steamers was keenly felt and was reflected in Dr Donald Anderson's editorial in the Autumn 1966 issue of *Ship Ahoy*:

> *As the season comes to its close coastal steamship operators must surely be glad of the prospect of the winter respite in order to lick their wounds. This can hardly have been a happy year, with the seamen's strike, small boat disasters and the appalling, mid-season weather discouraging many passengers.*
>
> *Minds will already be turning to 1967. What are the factors, general and local, which will affect next seasons operations What will be the effect of the £50 overseas travel allowance? Will this upset the mushrooming cross-channel ferry operators? Will it boost the strictly coastal trade if more folk take their holidays at home? Will the economic 'Squeeze', on the other hand, result in a shortage of cash for pleasure spending, particularly affecting those companies operating from industrial areas where unemployment is expected to rise? Can bankers continue to make the necessary credit available to tide operators over their 1966 losses? In the Bristol Channel, what will be the effect of the new Severn Bridge? Whatever 1967 holds it promises to be bedevilled with many an uncharted reef. It could well be that we will lose out on our diminishing fleet of paddle steamers!*

Down Below on the *Cardiff Queen*, Sunday 18 September 1966

The engine room. (Chris Collard)

The engine room alleyway looking forward. At the bottom centre can be seen the raised covering over the paddle shaft. Right of this is the paddle door, securely screwed closed, but which could be opened to allow access to the paddle wheel. (Chris Collard)

The forward tea saloon. (Chris Collard)

Outside the dining saloon; on the left is the bronze staircase inherited form the paddle steamer Westward Ho *after her breaking up in 1946.* (Chris Collard)

The dining saloon. (Chris Collard)

Nearing the end of her career, the Cardiff Queen *arrives at Mumbles Pier, from Swansea, bound for Ilfracombe and Padstow, Sunday 11 September 1966.* (Chris Collard)

1967/1968 – Finished With Engines

The Chairman's report to the shareholders at the AGM in January of 1967 stated:

> *It is regretted that the operation of two paddle steamers, as well as a screw vessel, in the Bristol Channel is no longer economic and the* Cardiff Queen *has, in consequence, been withdrawn from service.*

The company offered her for sale initially at £30,000; (she cost £144,000 to build in 1947), and every effort was made to find her gainful employment. Enquiries from River Cruises (Scotland) Ltd, concerning her possible use on the Firth of Forth, came to nothing and she remained laid up at Cardiff while the 1967 season was maintained by the *Bristol Queen* and the *Westward Ho*, the latter beginning service on the ferry in cold, windy weather on Maundy Thursday 23 March.

The novelty of travel over the Severn Bridge, via the new motorway, coupled with the very competitive road fares had, as feared, an immediate, adverse effect on the traffic from Cardiff to Weston.

This was particularly unfortunate as 1967 marked the 100th anniversary of Birnbeck Pier. A number of events were arranged to commemorate its opening, on 5 June 1867, by seven-year-old Cecil Hugh Smyth-Pigott, son of the Lord of the Manor. One of those events took place on the evening of Thursday 8 June when the *Westward Ho* ran a special cruise from Cardiff to Weston and around Steep Holm. She displayed the colourful elegance of a bygone era with many of her passengers wearing Victorian dress to celebrate the occasion.

In mid-April the *Bristol Queen's* overhaul was halted by a strike of Cardiff dock workers. She was towed to Avonmouth for it to be completed there but she was declared 'black' and had to be towed back to Cardiff. The work was completed by special arrangement with the dockers in time for her to begin her season on Monday 10 May.

During the winter, as part of her quinquennial survey, a considerable amount of work had been done on her paddles in the hope of alleviating the problems of recent years. She had also been fitted with radar, housed in a box-like structure, surmounted by the scanner, on the bridge.

The weather, during the early part of the season, was particularly wet but a fine spell in May coincided with the *Bristol Queen's* Isles of Scilly trip which she accomplished, without incident, between Saturday 13 May and the following Monday.

Despite her major winter maintenance she began to experience paddle trouble in early July and, as a precaution, her speed was reduced by an overall ten per cent to minimise the strain on her paddles. The first serious problem occurred on Friday 21 July when two radius rods fractured on a trip to Minehead. She made her way to Cardiff where she was repaired overnight.

Similar problems arose at Swansea on Thursday 3 August when she had to return up channel to the Roath Basin at Cardiff for repairs which kept her out of service for two days.

She was in dock again in mid-August but matters came to a head on Saturday 26 August when, off Barry, her starboard paddle struck submerged debris which caused considerable damage. She limped into Cardiff where, following an inspection, she was withdrawn from service.

The *St Trillo* was sent for immediately and arrived in Cardiff on the following day, when she took over the ferry, allowing the *Westward Ho* to take the *Bristol Queen's* sailings. The North Wales service was suspended for a week while arrangements were made for the charter of the Isles of Scilly Steamship Co.'s motorvessel *Queen of the Isles* which journeyed to North Wales to resume the sailings, in place of the *St Trillo*, from Monday 4 September.

In the meantime the *Bristol Queen* had entered the Queen Alexandra Dock, Cardiff, on Tuesday 29 August; her future uncertain.

At the board meeting on Wednesday 8 November Mr Smith-Cox reported that the 1967 season did not come up to expectations. Traffic from Ilfracombe had been good, Swansea and district fair, but from Cardiff, especially on the ferry, it had been poor. He estimated that at least three quarters of party traffic normally carried on the ferry had been conveyed by road over the Severn Bridge.

He also stated that the work done on the *Bristol Queen's* paddle wheels, including anealing, crack detecting and replacement of defective parts, had not proved satisfactory. Repairs to the damage sustained on 26 August would, alone, cost £8,000, and to make good all the defects of both wheels would cost in the region of £18,000. It was decided that it was not an economic proposition to put her into service again and steps should be taken for her disposal. It was agreed that no offer for scrap should be accepted until after 31 December 1967, in order to give an opportunity for her disposal at a better price.

In his Chairman's report to the shareholders Mr Smith-Cox stated:

'It is with regret that your directors have taken steps to dispose of both the *Bristol Queen* and *Cardiff Queen*. The operation of this type of ship has now become thoroughly uneconomic and it is no longer practicable to keep them in service.'

The broker's advertisement for the two steamers included the following:

> *We would refer to previous circulars advising that we could offer the* Cardiff Queen *for sale. We have now received instructions to offer a similar vessel, the* Bristol Queen...
>
> *It is understood that nearly £30,000 was spent this year in connection with load line survey and in renewals and improvements which included extensive re-tubing of the boiler, together with complete overhauls of machinery and auxiliaries... The vessel has certain paddle damage which the owners do not propose to repair. Specification for this repair is available and will be passed on to the purchaser...*
>
> *Both vessels are offered strictly 'as lies'... The owners have not indicated any price for the* Bristol Queen *but we would be pleased to try them with an offer in the region of £20,000. For the* Cardiff Queen *we would like to try the owners with an offer of around £15,000.*

The *Bristol Queen*, lying in a corner of the Queen Alexandra Dock, was badly damaged on Saturday 14 January 1968 when she was struck by the Liberian tanker *Geodor*, manoeuvring with tugs in high winds. The *Bristol Queen's* foremast stays were torn out, the mast snapped like a twig and fell into the dock. Her starboard bow, bulwarks and bridge wing were extensively damaged. Efforts to convert her into a floating museum and moves to preserve her engines came to nothing. She was purchased by Belgian shipbreakers and left Cardiff, in tow of the German tug *Fairplay X1*, on the afternoon of Wednesday 21 March 1968. She arrived at Ostend on Sunday 25 March and was handed over to the breakers at Flushing on the following day.

The *Cardiff Queen* was purchased early in 1968 by John Critchley, the owner of a number of

'DIY' and Government Surplus stores. His intention was to convert her into a floating nightclub, with dining facilities for 200 people, two dance floors, a swimming pool and a casino!

She was towed from the Graving Dock at Barry, where she had lain since June 1967, at 05.30 on Wednesday 29 February 1968, three days after the 21st Anniversary of her launch. Several hours later she was moored at Mill Parade Wharf, Newport; just upstream from the Transporter Bridge on the west bank of the River Usk, and adjacent to Mr Critchley's Newport premises. The derelict nature of the wharf caused her to break away from her moorings on the falling tide and slide, almost broadside, across the river, with four of Mr Critchley's employees aboard. During the course of the day arrangements were made for towage, but in the meantime nothing more could be done. The four stranded men lit a stove on the main deck to keep warm but were without food or drink. Eventually a volunteer braved the thigh-deep River Usk mud to take them fish and chips and flasks of hot tea and coffee which they hoisted on board in a bucket.

On the fast flowing flood tide she refloated and swung around, fortunately held by her two anchors and two remaining bow ropes. Later that evening she was towed into the South Dock, Newport, where she was allowed to remain for a few weeks while an alternative berth was sought. The mishap involved Mr Critchley in additional insurance and towage charges of over £3,000, and repairs to the Mill Parade Wharf were expected to cost over £10,000. These unforseen expenses, in addition to the estimated £40,000 for her conversion made the whole project untenable. A proposed public appeal to raise funds did not materialise and no alternative berth could be found. The venture was, therefore, abandoned. A few weeks later she was sold to the Newport shipbreakers, John Cashmore & Sons Ltd, and was towed to their yard on the afternoon of Tuesday 9 April 1968, where she was moored alongside the partially demolished frigate, *Ursa*. The workmen set about the breaking up of the *Cardiff Queen* on Wednesday 1 May 1968 and within a matter of weeks she was reduced to nothing more than a pile of scrap metal lying on the quayside. The last vestiges of the White Funnel paddle steamers had gone!

The Cardiff Queen *aground in the River Usk, Newport. Wednesday 29 February 1968.* (Chris Collard Collection)

Index

Numbers in italics refer to photographs

The Last Years of the White Funnel Paddle Steamers

All Photographs by Chris Collard

Aboard the Bristol Queen *in 1966.*

The Bristol Queen *at Hotwells Landing Stage. June 1967.*

The Bristol Queen *arriving at Weston in the 1960s.*

Capt. Power signals the Bristol Queen's *departure from Barry in June 1967.*

The Bristol Queen *in Minehead harbour, 1966.*

The Bristol Queen *at anchor off Lundy, June 1967.*

The Bristol Queen *arriving at Padstow in 1967.*

The Bristol Queen *at Hughtown, St Mary's, Isles of Scilly, Sunday 14 May 1967.*

The Bristol Queen *at Swansea, July 1967.*

The Bristol Queen *leaving Porthcawl in the 1960s.*

The Bristol Queen *in the Cumberland Basin, July 1967.*

The Bristol Queen *laid up in the Queen Alexandra Dock, Cardiff, in early March 1968. The damage inflicted by the Liberian tanker,* Geodor, *can clearly be seen.*

The Bristol Queen *leaving Cardiff for the breaker's yard, Wednesday 21 March 1968.*

The Bristol Queen *leaving Cardiff for the breaker's yard, Wednesday 21 March 1968.*

The Cardiff Queen *arriving at Weston in 1963.*

The Cardiff Queen *at Ilfracombe in 1964.*

The Cardiff Queen *embarking passengers at Clovelly, 1964.*

Aboard the Cardiff Queen *in heavy seas on the way from Lundy to Ilfracombe in 1965.*

Above and next: The Cardiff Queen *in the south lock at Newport, on her way to the breaker's yard, on Tuesday 9 April 1968.*

The Cardiff Queen *in the River Usk, nearing the end of her final journey.*

The Cardiff Queen *passing beneath the transporter bridge on her way to Cashmore's Yard, Tuesday 9 April 1968.*

The Cardiff Queen *at Cashmore's yard. April 1968.*

The Cardiff Queen *being broken up at Cashmore's yard, May 1968.*

Epilogue

On 1 January 1889 Peter and Alexander Campbell transferred their steamer business from the River Clyde to the Bristol Channel. The variety and efficiency of their services, with their expanding fleet of luxuriously appointed vessels, ensured that the White Funnel Fleet eventually eclipsed all of its competitors. Even two World Wars and the intervening years of the depression could not daunt the spirit of enterprise and determination which characterised all the company's endeavours.

The 'Indian Summer' of the 1960s culminated in traumatic events which would have crushed many another steamship operator but which were faced with admirable fortitude.

Life had changed much during the course of the company's history, but the popularity of the 'boat trip' had endured. Ultimately, it was the harsh realities of economics which caused the demise of the two *Queens* after their tragically short lives, bringing to an end the long line of paddle steamers which had graced the waters of the Bristol Channel for so long.

The company continued its services for over ten years using a variety of motor vessels. Their economy of operation made them more financially viable but the ships themselves lacked the appeal and the charisma of the paddle steamers. Gone were the spacious decks, the reassuring, rhythmic beat of the paddles and the hypnotic fascination of the engines in motion.

For many people it was hard to accept that the paddle steamers were no more; they had become so much a part of the summer scene on the shores of the Bristol Channel and a day at the seaside rarely passed without a sight of one or more of them.

However, the sad fact remained that their era had passed and the tradition which the Campbell brothers began eighty years before had ended.

The days of the White Funnel paddle steamer were over.